T0234554

The Insider Threat

The Insider Threat

Assessment and Mitigation of Risks

Eleanor E. Thompson

CRC Press
Taylor & Francis Group
Boca Raton London New York

CRC Press is an imprint of the
Taylor & Francis Group, an **informa** business

AN AUERBACH BOOK

CRC Press
Taylor & Francis Group
6000 Broken Sound Parkway NW, Suite 300
Boca Raton, FL 33487-2742

First issued in paperback 2021

ISBN-13: 978-1-4987-4708-0 (hbk)
ISBN-13: 978-0-367-56530-5 (pbk)

Visit the Taylor & Francis Web site at
http://www.taylorandfrancis.com

and the CRC Press Web site at
http://www.crcpress.com

Dedicated to those who have the perseverance and heart to be an organizational change agent; it is with you that I stand by for heavy rolls as the ship comes about.

Contents

Acknowledgments

A world of thanks to my resiliency team Anthony Alarid, Elena Hughes, Eric Lablance, Grace Soto, Jonathan Kincaid, and Kofi Aboagye; I am truly lucky to have you as my dearest friends and mentors. Thank you to my former academic team Dr. Robert Levasseur, Dr. Elizabeth Hagens, and Dr. Anne Hacker. Thank you to my publishing agent Rich O'Hanley for being so patient. Thank you to William "Dean" Lee for letting me get to work all those years ago. Thank you to my numerous shipmates and colleagues who have allowed me to ask a lot of questions and bounce ideas especially Russell Watkins, Jonathan Kincaid, Christopher Thomas, Anthony Alarid, Darek Kitlinski, Nathan Hall, Knud Foss, and Mark Logan. To my creative children Carlton Coughlin, Shannon Thompson, Meredith Thompson—imagine, imagine. Finally to my spouse Shay Spivey away, away, on the high seas.

Author

Eleanor E. Thompson, PhD, is known as an organizational change agent, and in 2016 was awarded the U.S. Coast Guard Commandant's Superior Achievement Award for cybersecurity innovation. After conducting a groundbreaking sociological study on an information technology problem—Insider Threat—Dr. Thompson applied her research to transform the U.S. Coast Guard toward a vision for operating in the cyber domain. Dr. Thompson has a 20-plus year career history with the U.S. Coast Guard and has worked at the senior-most levels as a policy and operations advisor, including on the commandant's staff (Tom Collins and Thad Allen), as well as advising those who would become commandant (Robert Papp).

During a historical post–9/11 effort by the government to both create and improve homeland security, Dr. Thompson served as a U.S. delegate to a specialized forum of the United Nations—the International Maritime Organization—located in London, UK, for the assembly, council (lead for Coast Guard), and technical cooperation committee (lead for Coast Guard). Notable achievements included furthering the adoption and implementation of the International Ship and Port Facility Security (ISPS) Code, which came into force in 2004, along with the U.S. implementation of ISPS as the Maritime Transportation Security Act of 2002/2004 (MTSA), first enacted by the 107th Congress to address port and waterway security, and signed by President George W. Bush in November 2002. Her writings were incorporated into presidential documents including the US-EU Declaration on Combatting Terrorism (June 2004). Dr. Thompson served as a member of the transition team to stand up U.S. Department of Homeland Security and participated in subsequent quadrennial Homeland Security reviews, as well as development of the International Port Security Program.

Dr. Thompson has since supported numerous public–private partnership forums for the U.S. Coast Guard, for the deputy commandant for operations, both domestically and internationally, furthering U.S. strategic objectives through negotiations, and promoting concepts such as homeland security; maritime domain awareness; maritime security; awareness of the U.S. as an Arctic nation; critical infrastructure protection; and cybersecurity. Her writings have been directly incorporated or adopted by two U.S. presidents, George W. Bush and President Barack Obama; three secretaries of the Department of Homeland Security (DHS), including Tom Ridge, Michael Chertoff, and Janet Napolitano; four U.S. Coast Guard commandants, including those previously mentioned, and Paul Zukunft; two U.S. secretaries of state, including Colin Powell and Condoleezza Rice; two Transportation Security Administration (TSA) administrators, including Kip Hawley and John Pistole, and numerous other senior executives and flag officers, two who have gone on to lead the TSA (Peter Neffenger and David Pekoske). Dr. Thompson's writings have focused on commitment to counterterrorism; developing and establishing the U.S. Coast Guard Cyber Command; promoting maritime security response operations post–9/11; developing strategy including cyber strategy, Arctic strategy, and Western Hemisphere strategy; as well as other U.S. Coast Guard and TSA mission and support topics, such as human capital strategy.

Dr. Thompson has extensive experience with the development of national plans including the National Infrastructure Protection Plan (NIPP), the Transportation System Sector-Specific Plan (TS SSP), and various Presidential Policy Decision Directives relating to critical infrastructure and resilience (such as HSPD-7/PPD-21, PPD-8, and EO 13636). She has experience in national-level pandemic response (e.g., H1N1) and reducing risk from all hazards, natural and man-made—with a focus on physical, cyber, and human risk elements.

Early in her career, she supported the Coast Guard Atlantic area and district commanders, and specifically as an advisor to the Atlantic area chief of operations, and Fifth District Operations chief as an operations analyst, where she managed Coast Guard Operation Sail 2000 participation/planning/security and helped to develop the initial concept of the deployable operations group among other operations. She is also a graduate of the U.S. Coast Guard Officer Candidate School, Yorktown, Virginia, and last class 3-98 that turned out the lights. She has served onboard an operational medium endurance cutter as the communications officer, intercepting go-fasts and conducting law enforcement operations on the Spanish Main.

Dr. Thompson holds an associate degree in applied criminal justice; a BS in sociology; a master's degree in public administration (justice administration), all from Columbus State University, Georgia. She also holds a master's degree in human resource management from Troy State University, Alabama, and a PhD in public policy and administration (information technology security and management) from Walden University, Minnesota. She has been an associate faculty member for over a decade for the University of Phoenix—Online and Northern Virginia Campus—where she is also a subject matter expert for curriculum development for both criminal justice and security in critical infrastructure protection and cyberspace, as well as for network security in information systems and technology.

Originally from Ottawa, Ontario, Canada, Dr. Thompson now calls Virginia home. She remains dedicated to the missions of the U.S. Coast Guard and continues to support the chief information officer and chief information security officer as a civil servant in Washington, DC.

1

INTRODUCTION

1.1 Introduction

This book is all about the *Insider Threat: Assessment and Mitigation of Risks*. It is part of a very important cyberspace story that impacts you—no matter who you are or where you are geographically located, on land, rocking on the high seas, flying through the air, or on the next space mission to Mars. One is hard-pressed to find any individual who does not have access to or connections with any organization or business. Even children connect; these connections are occurring earlier and earlier in life. So essentially, this book applies to you in your professional, personal, and spiritual life. Consider that you are your own asset and that your existence today and your potential should be viewed as an asset of your future. Consequences of insider threat can gravely damage this future; insider threat can come at a cost to you and you must mitigate against this risk. Insider threat is also significantly greater because of the lightning speed of damaged reputations, potential financial, material, and other losses.

This is a narrative on insider threat; assessment and mitigation of risks is a story that should be told, a story that I feel compelled to tell for the common good, so that you and others may incorporate your perspectives, protect your organizations, and grow the existing body of knowledge even further. It is also my hope that you will also use the knowledge gained to better protect yourself, as an asset, as well as your family members.

This is a unique story grounded in subject matter expertise and in part derived from an innovative qualitative study that uncovered some chilling results about the reality of insider threat. I've concluded that the best thing to do is to present for your consumption what I have come to know. I don't know all that you will take away, but am confident you will have an enlightened perspective when you have completely read this book. I have attempted to make this enjoyably readable, because there is a lot of confusing, less-informed, redundant, and quite frankly difficult material to read out there. I have also tried to make it somewhat entertaining, but there are no false stories here. What I am to share is so much more than the current body of knowledge, and significantly more than when I started on this journey of interest and quest for knowledge.

This book is informed by my original works—a qualitative research study as a foundation, but it takes on a greater depth of the understanding about insider threat; assessment and mitigation of risks. This knowledge on insider threat is provided on the one hand for the sake of learning, and on the other hand for the value of storytelling, which can be a mitigation tool itself—awareness of scenarios, best practices, and lessons learned. I'm grateful for the opportunity to be able to share this story with others, and the lessons I have learned along the way that got me here. It is important that individuals and organizations each come to better understand insider threat, to protect best interests, and the interests of others in business practice.

This book will be readable and informative, and ever so slightly entertaining to most. Every time I attend a conference or workshop on insider threat and listen to the speakers on this topic, I want to shout out "you are missing part of the story," and yet I know that I hold part of this story. I can't hold onto it, nor do I want to for much longer. This story belongs to more than me, my practitioner experiences, or my academic undertaking, and even my school of hard knocks—I have a few of them that hit me fairly hard right in the gut, or I suppose the heart—greatly contribute to this undertaking. If vignette stories you find off putting, just note that for without them, I don't think I would have made it through the writing of this book.

Logistically, because my primary income is derived from the U.S. federal government, specifically the U.S. Coast Guard where I work as a cybersecurity strategist and advisor to the chief information security officer, I must disclose the following: This book is an original work. The views expressed herein are those of the author and are not to be construed as official or reflecting the views of the commandant or of the U.S. Coast Guard. This book was not developed in consultation with the Coast Guard, but parts of the text may have been drawn from my professional life experiences, which include my role as a federal civil service employee working for the Coast Guard,

U.S. Department of Homeland Security. I am also an associate faculty member for a private university in the college of information systems and technology and criminal justice. These roles are complementary from a practitioner-academic learning perspective. The views expressed are also not considered official views or reflect views of this or any other private organization.

Additionally, the purpose and scope of this book is significantly different from a qualitative research study that I published in 2014 as an academic venture, focused on investigating the phenomenon of unintended insider threat and contributed to the theoretical literature of insider threat. In that self-funded academic study, the Coast Guard was a community research partner, but for which those views, as stated in the study, were also not to be construed as official or reflecting views of the commandant or of the Coast Guard.

I would like to stipulate that some of the knowledge learned, including several categorical findings, have been applied to inform the development of this book, especially the theoretical underpinnings in the information technology security that remained limited before that original study. The new sociological lens acquired during the 2014 study, as well as my ongoing experience in the field of cybersecurity and applied leadership in the organizational transformation that include cybersecurity response and remediation, has matured the topic in cybersecurity. It is, however, important to note the conceptual framework that inspired my study and for which I have added to the body of the literature since that time.

In 1992, Loch, Carr, and Warkentin identified threats to information systems in four dimensions, which included (1) *sources* that were internal or external; (2) *perpetrators* that were either human or nonhuman, and that could originate from either internal or external sources; (3) *intent* that was either accidental or intentional and could originate from human or nonhuman perpetrators, and that may be introduced by internal or external sources; and (4) *consequences* that included disclosure, modification destruction or denial of use and are as a result of either accidental or unintentional intent, which originates from either human or nonhuman perpetrators and may be introduced by internal or external sources.[1]

I used this conceptual framework to inform my original study, and as a result of my study, I proposed that a fifth and sixth category be added as *mediums* and *enforcers*. Mediums are the convergence points or crossroads where the internal and external source connects—as the doorway, an in between. A convergence may occur in between numerous internal and external pathways, created by humans and nonhumans. The risks, vulnerabilities, consequences, and mitigation measures will vary and need to be considered from a convergence perspective between the in and out. Opportunity exists to mitigate risk at the crossroads and prevent threat from becoming realized. Enforcers may be responding or policing, and are either human or nonhuman in the pragmatic of resilient countermeasures derived from analytic tools, risk management process, technological, or other human instruments that can originate from internal or external sources. The conceptual framework could then be reordered as a foundation to be sources, mediums, perpetrators, intent, enforcers, and consequences.

The concept of risk includes the possibility and probability of a particular event occurring. Loch et al. further describe the manifestation, extent, and severity of the consequences that are connected to the probability and the modifying factors. Modifying factors are seen as the internal and external influences that the probability will actually happen. Loch et al. categorized modifying factors for internal threats as employee acts and administrative procedures; for external threats, competitors and hackers. It is this work that I have expanded upon, but you should be aware of its existence as an important conceptual framework.

Researchers Warkentin and Willison have indicated that maturity in a given field is gained as study increases and there is a shift of scope from the technical to the organizational or managerial, and this book demonstrates, in part, that maturation process.[2]

It is time to look upon the face of what insider threat actually is, to incorporate better practices for the assessment and mitigation of risks, as well as to understand more holistically what insider threat actually is in practice. The more well-known category of malicious insider is only one primary category. The insider threat, through our actions or in-actions, dwell in each of us, and in everyone we connect with, in one way or another—and I have identified several specific categories discussed later in this book that may be addressed at an individual and managerial level to reduce risk and preserve your future.

I started this journey, as adventures often start, by being curious. This particular journey has led me much further into an adventure quest than I had anticipated. It is this knowledge that I share throughout this book. I have combined a sociological approach to an information technology problem. What has emerged is truly eye opening and useful to a wide breadth of stakeholders including the chief executive officer, chief information officer, chief information security officer, professional protection officers, organizational security managers, supervisors, and general managers as well as other practitioners, students, and individuals as lifelong learners.

Make haste! As you have likely observed, you are in it—virtually and physically in it—and together, we are in the cybersecurity time of our lives. With technology, this time could potentially be infinite, even lasting beyond our physical forms as our intellectual capital may take a life of its own. We exist in a crescendo of technological advances and a flurry of communications. We must not only make sense of the sensory madness but also ensure that we have a solid grasp on security technology, all the while maintaining a firm grasp on traditional security practices. Practical application of organizational security risk management is necessary for organizations to survive and thrive in a globally competitive, highly visible, and nearly unforgiving social media environment.

The need for increased cybersecurity to reduce insider threat is also soundly upon us. Almost every day there is a new story in the media being shared about another instance of an organizational compromise or intrusion impacting customers, employees, government, and other stakeholders. This intrusion or attack may have originated from within or be external to the organization; both can result in catastrophic consequences. However, to penetrate from outside the organization, it is likely that an insider created an opening for this to occur; this unsecured door or opening may have been created either intentionally or unintentionally. There is clearly a documented need for an increased focus on traditional and cybersecurity. Insider threat is an excellent place to start, that you may develop an insider threat program that addresses the assessment and mitigation of risk related to this threat.

Clearly, the rapid transformation of society into a digital culture has been on the upswing since the early 1990s, and it hasn't even slowed; evidence points to the fact that it will continue to grow exponentially. As a result of this rapid upswing, competency gaps were created within the workplace, partly because traditional college curriculums often failed to keep pace with the changes in interdisciplinary areas. In my opinion and through personal observation, they are now just starting to catch up, though not all of the professors have had the opportunity to self-develop in these complex technology disciplines, even at a strategic level. There are some exceptions where universities have established centers of excellence and partnerships with both industry and government in the area of cybersecurity. Even in practice, traditional security has at times been at arm's length with cybersecurity, when both should have been collaborating together a great deal more for a broader holistic security approach.

Since I am going to be forthright in this book, here it is—the need for increased information technology security arrived at least four decades ago. It is readily apparent that organizations just weren't in listening mode, or other priorities overshadowed these security decisions for lack of urgency, or decision makers were dialed into the wrong frequency. However, as time has progressed, and more cyber-havoc has been created, tremendous financial loss has occurred because of security mistakes inside the perimeter. A choice really doesn't exist now. There is so much threat, originating both internally and externally, that there has been a start to an ideological shift. More organizations and their leadership have recently, especially since 2015, realized that they must tune into the right cybersecurity frequency, metaphorically speaking, in order to hear the proper communications and filter out the competing background noise.

1.1.1 The Risk Landscape of Insider Threat

Risk landscapes are frequently developed in order to both describe and scope the unique characteristics of a given topic area, in the broader context of a particular situation, as applied to a particular geographic area (physical or virtual). For example, an organization or agency could develop a risk landscape that specifically applies insider threat, within the broader context of organizational risk within a particular industry, located within the United States, with accessibility from around the globe.

In well-known practice, the U.S. Department of Homeland Security, along with other agencies, develops risk landscapes and uses them to inform the strategists and others in the public and private sectors who create and inform various products and plans. These risk landscapes are often credited as providing a foundation for national level plans with impacts across infrastructure sectors. Risk landscapes can be considered the backstory along with articulating the general conditions that a government entity, particular industry segment, or sector must operate within. These are the known or expected conditions. They may predict a potential threat and speculate increased risk in the future, in general terms, or in projected/expected forecast.

Your specific insider threat landscape will vary slightly depending on your location, the nature of your business, and the potential known threats. You likely already have a baseline in place and some mitigating measures that address organizational risk, but you will have to conduct a deeper dive than that to then deduce other aspects of insider threat you likely have not considered. You may have some risk reduction mitigation measures already in place, either voluntary, being required by regulation, or other policies you must adhere to simply by local ordinance. For example, the risk of liability may be offset through various insurance policies. Later in the book, you will discover various insider threats that should be considered as you relook at your present landscape and reassess your mitigation of risks. Lack of proper understanding of the risk landscape that insiders present can create holes in your security fence—virtual cyber vulnerabilities however small, left unchecked, can have the consequences of a Grand Canyon opening. You need to protect your future by reducing the risk of insider threat, to reduce unwanted accessibility or your potential loss.

Typically, risk landscapes should be created to inform the decision making as well as the development of organizational products such as strategies, plans, projects, and blueprints. They help to shape prioritization of the assessment and mitigation of risk, and also help to inform decision makers at all levels. Many people are simply not aware of the landscape that personally impacts them. While the entire landscape will never be fully revealed, they can be developed to remove some of the blinders to contribute to a more optimal assessment. Landscapes should, whenever possible, incorporate aspects of physical, cyber, and human risk elements. Landscape development should also include a diversity of stakeholders. In the case of a business or organization, perspectives of individuals who are more junior in the organization may also bring a wealth of insight into the landscape. If only someone trusted would ask, and then be able to interpret the communicated perceived risks. As an associate faculty, I'm always amazed at the level of insight provided by my students who are often mid-level security personnel, including security guards; they have insights that are rarely filtered up to the senior level decision makers due to layers of bureaucracy.

It is best to remember that landscapes extend well beyond the horizon. Indeed, with today's technology it is a layered landscape that includes traditional security risk, but also cybersecurity risk. Multiple stakeholders or contributors can also be reviewers of this landscape built from various perspectives that help to refine it from their informed perspective. Not everyone can easily see the pitfalls that lay ahead—unexpected changes in technology security requiring significant investment like particular operating systems no longer supported making specialized custom software no longer usable—living downstream from a century-old dam having no alerts and warnings, for example. In some cases, a risk landscape can make a venture either a good idea or a not so good idea. That information technology investment in a major acquisition, for example, may not have had very good cybersecurity life cycle cost estimates when it was originally acquired. A current risk landscape can help determine what level of risk can be accepted, as well as the level of risk that needs to be specifically mitigated, even if a threat is an unknown factor or placeholder.

The formation of a risk landscape can also help to identify emergent needs to balance particular risks. For illustrative purposes, I use an example of a physical world risk of a subject matter area that I worked in during my earlier criminal justice studies in the mid-1990s. The example is that of a risk landscape with the presence of convicted sex offenders within a community. After much research, study, and experience in this field, I'm an advocate of simply locking up convicted child sex offenders and throwing away the key. However, public policy and judicial enforcement have not reached that level; therefore, sex offender registries have now been created in each state in part because some sex offenders become repeat sex offenders after they serve their prison time, and more public awareness of the increased threat posed by offenders, who could be living close to a school or even next door, is needed. Sex offenders may try to get employment positions with businesses that may have lax or improper screening processes, where they will have access to children. This is an extremely risky insider threat, where the exploitation of children would bring on significant liability to the business owner, or local governments if a government-run center. There is an illusion that all sex offenders are mean-spirited in disposition, when in contrast many sex offenders can be quite charming people—both male and female sex offenders; they can hide in the open under the guise of trust and authority positions until being caught.

Locate a state registry, enter your zip code or surrounding areas, and you can determine who your local convicted sex offenders are, keeping in mind these are only the offenders who have been convicted. There are likely to be many times this amount, and the unknown or estimated threat should still be factored into your landscape. Because of the severity of the risk landscape with high-profile cases that demonstrate the reality of criminal recidivism, the U.S. Department of Justice now manages a National Sex Offender Public Registry, which was renamed by the Adam Walsh Child Protection Safety Act of 2006 as the Dru Sjodin National Sex Offender Public Website (NSOPW). This public safety resource provides public access to sex offender data nationwide and is searchable through various search options, including the offender's name. Increased community awareness information is now available online, including by mobile application, by state, as well as from tribal lands—nationwide. The risk landscape has changed by layering technological applications so that now there is a heightened awareness. This awareness has the effect of not only alerting the community of pertinent safety precautions, which is a positive result, but impacts economic investment considerations, which could be a negative result. Registered sex offenders tend to cluster in particular areas because they can get housing. This can negatively impact business, residential value, and viability. For example, I owned a home in a neighborhood in Virginia about eight houses away from where two sex offenders moved in together to be roommates. I was no longer able to rent my home at market value to anyone with children. Actually, no one with children wanted to rent the home, even at discounted rates.

From a risk landscape perspective, during times of threat, the risk landscape should be reevaluated to see if something has changed. For example, in the case of a missing child, police officers may question sex offenders with convictions who may be at higher risk for recidivism of particular sex crimes given particular conditions. There are some sex offenders that may have been wrongfully convicted or convicted for a much-less-severe offense. For the sake of illustrated argument, the risk in the landscape for the individual who has served his or her judicial punishment is a continuous monitoring by the community of where they live and where they work. Every entity they connect with now has the ability to review their sex offender record. Now I'll shift to another risk landscape example.

In the late 1990s, one of my work projects required me to oversee the development of U.S. east coast security plans for port security in multiple ports for the summer of 2000. As a celebration of the new millennium, a parade of tall ships, with up to 200 vessels as parade participants including tall ships and warships, had been promoted as the largest peacetime assemblage of naval and training ships in history, and would include 70,000 smaller spectator pleasure crafts. Touted as the largest movement of ships since WWII; Walter Cronkite narrated the promotions for this multi-month eight-port spectacular event. One of the major ports included New York Harbor that concurrently held the high-profile International Naval Review. Whereas maritime risk assessments have significantly evolved in a post–9/11 environment, this earlier security assessment work was a solid foundation for assessing risk in the maritime domain. A more mature risk assessment process for port areas was later developed with extensive critical infrastructure input from multiple sectors, but still built from the ground level up and matured through evolving knowledge of the landscape, such as supply chain and security management, and prioritization of critical infrastructure protection/security.

Another example I was specifically involved in was the development of an event risk assessment for the port of Baltimore, including its inner harbor. During this assessment, it was determined that the maritime domain was not simply the waterways and channels but extended beyond to multiple stakeholders for a comprehensive understanding of the landscape. For example, what types of industry surrounded the port and was any of these industries hazardous? Further examinations considered if an accident occurred, man-made or otherwise, how far might the damage extend? Additionally, response times for emergency support were considered. Specific geographic locations incorporated local crime trends, the capacity of land, air and sea response was also important, along with consideration of additional protections for participants and spectators. This risk landscape might have included various weather conditions, daily temperatures, access of food venues for spectators, emergency exit routes, and establishing security perimeters for proximity to vessels, and even required notice of arrivals for vessels. Once the risk landscape was assembled, a matrix of scenarios that were specific to the port area were created based on this landscape and the subject matter experts from various local, state, and federal agencies as well as industry. The risk of these scenarios occurring, given the particular resources available was assessed in a basic formula of high, medium, and low risk as well as the impact ratio of these risks. This assessment was not conducted in a vacuum, industry and local governments were key stakeholders and intimately involved in this process.

As a result of this extensive risk assessment, various stakeholders could apply varying degrees of mitigation measures. It was also determined in this and other ports along the U.S. east coast, that additional event sponsor security was needed in multiple port areas, and that a Unified Command System was needed to assist in the management of an event of this scope and magnitude with event engagement required. The event sponsors agreed. A Unified Command is a component of the National Incident Command System structure that is used to respond to either planned or emergency events. It is an adaptable structure, frequently used by localities as well as state and national responders such as the Federal Emergency Management Agency (FEMA). There are basic training sessions that are openly available to the public; visit FEMA[3] online to determine what free trainings are available to you.

Additionally, a temporary rule was created so that ships coming into the ports would be required to give notice further in advance of their arrival. That rule, post–9/11, has since been permanently modified to require further advance notice of arrival. The increased threat of terrorism, and heighted risk against the United States required many regulatory changes not just in the United States but also around the globe.

The development of a more extensive risk assessment model, called the Maritime Security Risk Analysis Model (MSRAM), was developed by the Coast Guard and remains in place today. The model has been shared with several agencies and departments for separate development. The desirability of this model is that it is created from both a ground up and top down approach, it is adaptable and continually changing. The existence of this model has been shared openly. Where I am not able to discuss the model methodology in entirety, the model is scenario based and incorporates a vast amount of information from across multiple critical infrastructure sectors that overlap in the Maritime Transportation System. It is an adaptable model to changing threats and assessments.

If a large organization, small business, or individual has a limited understanding of their risk landscape, it is time to build a risk landscape that should also factor in the landscape insider threat. This landscape will change over time and should be adaptable. Consider an individual who purchases a home in a particular area. This area continues to grow, but the transportation systems to support this area remain the same, and the responder capabilities are not funded at higher levels. In the event of an incident that requires emergent response, police and ambulance response times will be reduced and traffic barriers may exist for an individual to reach emergency services themselves with gridlocked traffic. If an individual has a health risk, it might be time to relocate their housing to an area where lifesaving services may be more easily reached, try to influence the development of more emergency services, or have other lifesaving aids such as a home care worker. Bringing a worker into a home creates additional insider threat—the more people with access or connectivity, the greater the threat. While this is a more basic scenario it shows how factors in a risk landscape can inform an assessment and subsequent mitigation of risk. A risk landscape can be defined as a system of systems and conditions interacting, that inform the assessment and mitigation of risk of a particular individual, business, or organization.

A best practice for any organization is to understand what their risk landscape looks like. Although intelligence can be used to inform these products at a national level, this does not mean that other very relevant information can't be obtained through open source, if this access is not available. Historically the United States gathered intelligence by being in listening mode, but now intelligence can be gathered and compiled more openly through various online sources. An organization can easily create similar constructs. Compiling various pieces of open source information, to include academia, business sector, and government can soon create an accurate risk landscape, and useful picture for the assessment and mitigation of risk for the organization. Some organizations, depending on their nature, may even be able to become part of a partnership with governments and gain even more relevant information about potential threats. Sharing of this information among stakeholders is challenging, individuals representing their organizations have provided this collaboration in the past and have also become vulnerable to data loss by the federal government.

Whereas risk landscapes can be very strategic in nature, they will also include very specific focus areas if selected, such as the risk landscape of insider threat. This risk landscape should inform organizational risk assessments and allow decision makers the autonomy to decide if the identified risk should ultimately be "mitigated, avoided, accepted or transferred,"[4] and importantly the prioritization of such efforts.

Private and public sector approaches to risk management tend to vary because of differences in their enterprise approaches. Whereas the private sector may focus on "shareholder value, efficacy, and customer service,"[5] the public sector has a different scope of accountability for the public and more closely aligned with a defined mission and congressional accountability for that purpose. However, both should consider risk, including insider threat, because this is an area of risk for which they are both vulnerable. Contextually, in order to understand the elements, understanding assets and where they fit within the risk landscape is also critical.

Andrew Feenberg,[6] a world-renowned philosopher, publishing prior to and after the millennium, focused on *critical theory* and technology-related concepts. Very briefly, I interpreted part of his perspectives on critical theory to mean that technology has basically become so integrated into the fabric of society that it can be difficult to see where the technology begins or ends. I will later describe my findings that support this assertion. In some cases, it makes it quite difficult to assess the risk of technology, especially if it is not clearly understood where this technology exists, begins, and we as humans end. It is true that many people almost seem to have smart technology integrated into their bodies; for example, the smartphone becomes an extension of their fingers. This can make assessing and mitigating risk a challenge, but not impossible. Being able to see past these ideological blinders will take some practical awareness and practice. There is a body of literature, this book included, that will help guide you to gaining a greater depth into insider threat; assessment and mitigation of risks.

It is good to continually challenge the assumptions and to critically think how you can challenge these assumptions. For example, if you believe that something is—always one way or another—this may be a red flag, and perhaps it is better to come to understand that something might be always one way or another—until one day it isn't. Think ideological emancipation. How can you think to free yourself from your own way of thinking?

As an initial resource, and holder of various parts of the puzzle, I point in the direction of the United States Computer Emergency Readiness Team, also known as US-CERT, which is a function of the Department of Homeland Security and promotes that it "leads to improve the Nation's cybersecurity posture, coordinate cyber information sharing, and proactively manage cyber risks to the Nation."[7] Although not consolidated into a specific risk landscape document, there are many clues about the current state of the cybersecurity environment that can be used to inform general activities of the risk landscape. This resource should be visited frequently to determine emergent issues or concerns.

1.1.2 The Ground Truth of Insider Threat

Insider threat is not an abstract phenomenon in technology; it has now taken on a higher level of concern. However, it is still not often understood how good people can be insider threats. I have identified human behavior, through qualitative study, that demonstrates the real insider threat that includes both intended and unintended threats. I will begin by sharing the four types of insider threats that I have categorized. There are four types of organizational insider threats that point to every employee, and those with connections. They are: the *virtuous insider,* the *wicked insider,* the *vengeful insider,* and the *malicious insider* (Figure 1.1).

Often the virtuous and the wicked insiders are left out of the literature, or simply marginalized. These are very important aspects of

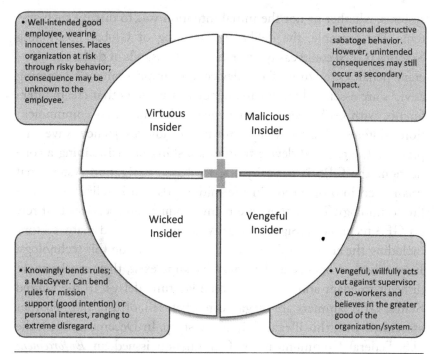

- Well-intended good employee, wearing innocent lenses. Places organization at risk through risky behavior; consequence may be unknown to the employee.

- Intentional destructive sabotoge behavior. However, unintended consequences may still occur as secondary impact.

Virtuous Insider

Malicious Insider

Wicked Insider

Vengeful Insider

- Knowingly bends rules; a MacGyver. Can bend rules for mission support (good intention) or personal interest, ranging to extreme disregard.

- Vengeful, willfully acts out against supervisor or co-workers and believes in the greater good of the organization/system.

Figure 1.1 All insiders are a threat to organization.

insider threat and the foundation of insider threat within an organization. These good people create big holes in the perimeter fence that are left open, and if unchecked will eventually allow data to be released, where trespassers may retrieve data, or simply come in and observe what is going on. Since the majority of employees in an organization are likely to fit into this category, it is worth a much closer look.

Keep in mind that all insiders are a threat to organizations, each to varying degrees on the surface but having large risk factors. These situations will be explained in much detail further in the book. You have an opportunity to take this knowledge, to raise a higher visibility of this issue within your organization. Technology implications may be thought of as something that just the techies need to think about, and that it's outside of other operational concerns. This is simply not the case. I would speculate that you would be hard pressed to identify an element of the workforce or in your organization that does not rely on some form of technology.

Some employees may use technology illegally to get around a compliance system, and in doing so may actually disrupt other necessary systems, whether or not the initial intention was to disrupt such systems. For example, the deliberate jamming of Global Positioning Systems (GPS) could easily cause tens of thousands of dollars in monetary penalties, seizure of the device, and imprisonment.[8] Jamming devices are essentially radio-frequency transmitters that create interference with GPS systems, Wi-Fi networks, and other communications systems. This works by emitting a radio-frequency wave that prevents the targeted device from establishing or maintaining a connection. The GPS is basically a space-based navigation system that was placed into operation in the mid-1990s and is reliant on satellite technology. Today there are many products and services that rely on GPS technology. Signal integrity is important, and many sectors, including the emergency services sector are reliant on this technology. Even when secondary and tertiary backups exist, they can be more difficult to adapt and can cause some lag time delays. In the United States, GPS jammers are illegal to market, sell, or use, and penalties associated with this illegal activity are steep. In December, 2014, the U.S. Federal Communications Commission issued an *Enforcement Advisory* as a warning to the general public. Only federal agencies are able to apply for and receive authorization to use jammers. However, despite these restrictions, jamming may still occur and in some cases has been attributed to workers avoiding real-time detection by their employers. Slackers or shirkers are among those who resist being monitored.

In today's workplace, GPS trackers may be used for transportation systems to manage a fleet of delivery trucks. These illegal jammers could be viewed as seemingly harmless to the driver trying to avoid detection by his supervisors, but using a jammer that is not harmless creates other problems for necessary devices on emergency vehicles or other transportation modes reliant on satellite-based signals. Insider threat concerns everyone, and it's every employee's responsibility to more fully understand their role and how they can contribute to mitigate this risk; however, many personnel systems and core competencies have not yet embraced the current era of risk management as related to technology. Technologies may be very integrated and not clearly show the cascading impacts. Although the Federal Communications Commission has issued a warning and set up a tip hotline, this warning may not fully reach its intended audience. If an organization uses

GPS tracking, it would be a best practice to advise employees of their legal responsibilities as an employee, incorporating the prohibited use of jammers as a condition of employment and that use of such would be viewed as an insider threat. Training and workforce communications are necessary as transparency increasingly unfolds in the world of cybersecurity.

Many organizations exist today with an illusion of security, both virtual and physical. Illusions can create a false sense of security; this book is helping you to critically think your own organization. It is probably a matter of time where a security breach, traditional or cybersecurity is uncontrollably broadcast through the media, to competitors, and to current and potential customers that can quickly reduce profits, damage reputations, and potentially be devastatingly expensive to the organization, as well as individuals who are not fully protected under the organizational umbrella. Insider threat cases can have consequences that are equal in consumer perception to that of having a national restaurant chain sell contaminated food to patrons with the potential to cause death. The consequences, however, are not yet fully translatable in comprehension between the physical and cyber impacts and stories. If a vehicle is unable to start because a rogue employee maliciously disables a vehicle remotely, this could become a life or death situation, either placing the driver in a risky position or not allowing the driver to respond in an emergency situation. At minimum, the impact could be an organizational liability. A password hack by a former employee for an auto financing company in Texas, which used remote immobilization systems, reportedly led to over 100 cars being remotely disabled.[9]

The occurrences of insider threat and the need for sound decision-making and risk management have become increasingly necessary and highly visible, especially as media has highlighted individuals and organizations that have failed to take adequate protective measures and actions. Government and organizations have been slow to respond to cyber breaches, perhaps misinformation and half truths about cybersecurity and an over-reliance of existing cyber systems created a false sense of security, therefore being very misinformed about the issues of insider threat in particular. Understanding the depth of insider threat and aspects of assessment and mitigation of risk is certainly important. If you don't know what your assets actually are, or cannot account for your personnel and their behavior, the reality is that you are likely not measuring the right things and are making risk-based business decisions that are closer to junk science than being sound risk management choices.

Getting to know the reality of insider threat can be downright uncomfortable to our very nature of being, our friendships, and our careers. I believe that this book will be that type of awakening for you, will challenge your assumptions and force critical thinking and even behavior and organizational decision-making changes. I'll even share some personal observations that are on the edge of tabloid but demonstrate the risk we all take every day, and link that risk directly to insider threat. I might even feel slightly bad about using *executive shipwreck failure* examples; however, the concept of applying lessons learned and best practices is very important. It is easy to assume that your organization is using best practices, but the reality is that there is a lot to be learned out there in best practices. Executives that believe that these lessons learned are being reviewed and applied need a *trust-but-verify* sense of approach. Increased organizational accountability is essential for this practice. Knowledge management can be often stove-piped, and prohibitive of real growth and applied change management, stove-piped either by function or employee level, such as between management and line workers.

For some newsworthy and monumental executive shipwreck failures, such as was experienced by the U.S. Office of Personnel Management's (OPM) now-former director Katherine Archuleta,[10] we can assume that her cybersecurity ship has sailed, hit rocks, and sunk if we are being specific about the negative and unknown consequences to the federal workforce and volume of data compromise. I respect a professional who has reached career heights, often through hard work, but the landscape more often than not keeps changing, and one has to be continually aware of their surroundings, barely should they take the time to blink, without someone else covering for them, when holding such a position of trust. Archuleta resigned in July of 2015 after extreme pressure to do so, when she failed to secure the highly sensitive data of well over 20 million individuals; this highly sensitive data included biometric data, clearance interviews, social security numbers, and other information that was ultimately compromised because of poor cybersecurity hygiene practice.

If you have never gone through a security screening process before, I can tell you that this process reveals almost everything about a person, including in-depth interviews from former colleagues and neighbors, going back decades into the career of an individual. These investigations ask many questions and subsequently uncover anything that might be perceived as a compromise or threat to an individual, organization, or group. Only time will tell the effects and potentially negative consequences the compromised data will have on the impacted people. Many of these direct impacts will be difficult to map back to this breach. The response to provide credit monitoring alone as a solution and absent financial compensation, in my opinion, is completely inadequate.

The OPM hack was very calculated and deliberate, first finding a weakness in contractor security and then becoming a chameleon. Secure Sockets Layer (SSL) encryption had been used to cloak these deliberate activities; the false name for outbound traffic of opmsecurity. org had been used to deceive.[11] Through a series of standardized legitimate software products that OPM did not inherently use, malware had been hidden, thus giving the hackers clear access to OPM's servers.

One of the areas discovered in my personal research emphasized how time is very different in the land of cyber. Data can be stored for years, or simply continue to be collected over significant periods of time until the holder of this data determines a purpose for it. I expect that the ways this theft of public data will be used has yet to be imagined. Criminal organizations are not always in the business of destroying the networks they discover; instead they have an interest in exploiting them by harvesting or collecting data and information for future exploitation.

As technology changes, the power of this collected data, formed into meaningful packets of information, might become even more useful and of greater value. Much of this data theft, or data loss by the OPM, also included biometric data. Stolen biometric data could potentially be used against organizations because biometrics are often used in security access control. Especially with technological advances in Artificial Intelligence, the future use of this stolen data, and potential consequences are yet to be discovered.

Yes, this OPM breach I believe was absolutely preventable through higher levels of security requirements being placed into contracts and greater investment in cyber defense and offense, as well as employee awareness about insider threat. Each employee is an insider threat,

even at a virtuous or wicked level and must guard against complacency. During congressional testimony, it became increasingly clear
that Archuleta was not technologically savvy enough to understand
her core competency gaps. This cybersecurity breach contained current
and former federal workers sensitive data, their family information,
and even data on members of industry. This colossal failure comes at a
potentially high cost to millions of individuals where the extent of the
damage is not yet known. What resulted was a clear breach of government trust and a complete breakdown in basic cybersecurity hygiene
practice. In my previous interest and exploration, I have examined the
role of executives and their role in shaping the organizational culture
by looking both inward and outward. This experience by OPM should
be a lesson for many other agencies, a top priority in fact. However,
I would speculate that the lessons learned may be still slow in action
in several federal agencies.

I have come to realize, and even recommend, that terminating
individuals in these leadership positions is an acceptable cost to an
organization. Liability of damage must be mitigated and limited to
the maximum extent possible; the do-nothing attitude or resistant
response must not permeate the organization. Whether or not this
is a conscious decision by executives, or just an outcome of a situation is not fully understood, this is also a practice found. This is a
game of probability. For example, if hiring decisions are based on
perceived core cybersecurity competency rather than tested competency before hiring, or post-training competency testing, eventually
these shortcomings will catch up to an organization in compromises.
Cybersecurity has become a basic workforce competency. Insider
threat, and the prevention of it, is inherent to this competency, and
additional work must be done by the organization to assess and
mitigate insider threat risk. Developing a cyber-savvy workforce, at
large, is a good start.

So while the current practice continues, several careers have fallen
quickly and likely for a variety of decision-making reasons, but primarily because they did not understand the risk of insider threat in totality.
This limitation was likely in part because the literature has been historically incomplete, and also in part because executives did not look
inward long enough to understand the nature of their organization's
insider threat, nor come to understand the risk landscape that they

operated within. A risk landscape will continually change, and there are rarely restart buttons. These failed executives either were too busy to ask critical questions of their experts in staff, ignored research or advisement, and/or did not recruit or retain the talent that was needed for an effective cybersecurity strategy, specifically in the area of insider threat.

As mentioned, time does play a factor in another way, especially with technology security. Obsolescence is reached rather quickly. It is also likely in the time that it took to reach their executive peaks, the risk landscape that they had passed during their upward climb, with their topographical maps in hand, had become virtually obsolete. While they stood in their vista and looked forward, they forgot to look inward and continue their growth in the business competency area of basic cybersecurity hygiene practice and become cyber savvy. One person cannot be situationally aware everywhere physically or virtually, so executives and managers must pull a team together that can help them stay aware of the changing environment; and a team to help them brave the storm and watch for debris. *Damage control* is also very important, when suddenly and unexpectedly the executive is riding the ship that springs the leak. The reality is, right now, that is likely to occur. So having a damage control team either in-house or better yet on retainer will be fairly important. I am talking about preemptively developing and shaping resilience.

Literally, before our eyes—breach after breach, the executive management rules of the world are changing; like the photos you have seen of the house that didn't move, and the highway that was built around it. The highway is now virtual and we can't with our eyesight see the highway but it is there, everywhere. I'm sure the fallen were failed by others but sometimes taking the hit is the burden of being in charge. However, no matter the reason for failures, the challenges that executives, managers, and security officers face from both the public and private sector often include the struggle to understand insider threat and moreover, struggle to create a valid assessment and subsequent mitigation of risk as applied to their organizations or agencies. I have empathy, of course I do, but I am here to look at best practices and lessons learned and share them so that others may learn how to be more resilient, both individually and organizationally.

Technology continues to expand exponentially. To illustrate this fact, one just has to look at mobile telephone technology and how it has evolved over the last 20 years to understand the nature of technological change. These changes have occurred in a half generation, not in a century. Indeed we are on a fast path, but to where may be unclear, yet manageable. The digital divide is also narrowing due to the exponential expansion of mobile technology. More and more people around the globe have access, and at not just at a basic user level. This expansion introduces an entirely new layer of users from mobile technology, access, and applications. In 2015, hundreds of applications were removed from smartphone technology because of discovered security vulnerabilities that were linked to data-mining. The skill of those who use the technological systems has also changed. Children are now, metaphorically, born with an electronic tablet in their hands, long gone is the era of the silver spoon, unless there is an application for that. However, they are not born with the accompanying computer security book to help them understand the technology they are provided. I have found myself quieting children who are about ready to reveal their passwords openly to others.

The ground truth of insider threat is that you can learn more from your employees than you may realize. As an organization, functionally the right people need to be able to ask the right questions, to continually revisit the experts, to refine understanding and ask for clarification. If you identify that there is a gap in understanding and awareness, then it is time to look beyond your employees with other subject matter experts. Building a flexible and adaptable workforce in today's techno environment is very important. I have found, however, that a lot of outsourcing may occur before the internal saturation has been reached to get a more holistic understanding of the nature of insider threats. In retail establishments, it is commonly understood in the physical security protection community that employees who have the most access and understanding of an organization are more likely to steal products and/or other valuables than their customers. The employees are able to facilitate theft more easily from the inside as well, whether by providing extra unauthorized discounts to families or friends, or leaving off charges in order to gain a larger tip from an establishment that might pay the minimum wage, or even less, the server's base wage.

Even those experts who are consistently saturated with looking at insider threat and the assessment and mitigation of risk, the prospects of reducing this risk can be overwhelming. When I initially speak with someone who has little knowledge about insider threat, and even with experts who know a lot about insider threat, I first jump to discuss how insider threat is not presently described comprehensively in the literature and that its meaning has been scoped too narrowly because the perceived faraway espionage and malicious threat tends to be sexier than the reality of the holistic internal threat. I further explain, to those that want to have the dialogue, that there are some really important aspects to insider threat that have been erroneously set aside only to continue down a pathway of focusing on external risk. This is not to say that guarding against external threats is not important. It absolutely is—cybersecurity defense is important, but the approach needs to be applied in tandem, in order to reduce the external threats. The insider threat also needs to be reduced so that vulnerabilities may be collectively reduced and exposure minimized.

I am fortunate enough to have had the opportunity to be able to conduct research that fills in some of the knowledge gaps, actually quite a few as related to insider threat. Individuals and organizations should, for critical thinking purposes, set aside assumptions that insider threat is just an external force, or that their insider forces are only malicious or just erroneous—this isn't the case. There are both virtuous employees and wicked employees that really deserve additional attention at all levels of management within an organization. Cybersecurity is an entity responsibility. It should not be cast just into the chief information security officers' or chief information officers' bailiwick. Preconceived notions of responsibility should also be set aside along with definitions and understanding of *consequence*.

Consequences in the area of information technology security, is frequently not the same as a physical space consequence because the time element of the impact of a breach is not necessarily known immediately, and can be discovered well after the incident has occurred. Consequences in the cyber domain are often discovered long after initial compromises have occurred. Cyber breaches are making computer forensics an increasingly important field. Even with the sophisticated scanning technology of a well-organized cybersecurity watch, a breach discovery and follow-on consequences can have a significant delay.

Additionally, consequences can be created through technology that can't be detected or seen until the physical impacts happen and can be observed. With a larger disruption, they may be immediately observed, although this forensic digital evidence might need to be discovered to make this link. Causality may need to be established. Real-time monitoring can allow a faster response, to isolate a technological attack, and minimize cascading impact. Having a detection capability without a near real-time interdiction can be problematic as well. Monitoring should not simply occur Monday through Friday and then shut down after-hours or on the weekend; this is an illusion of cybersecurity. Knowing not only if someone has breached your system, but is still there collecting various types of data, systems should be monitoring us 24/7, year round. Also of significant importance is identifying what type of data was stolen, if it was likely targeted data, or happenstance.

More sophisticated and well-trained response teams can provide decoy information as a form of counterattack, while investigating the compromise without alerting the intruder. For example, if a competitor is trolling for intellectual capital, false prototypes or initiatives could also be released or made easily accessible. This, however, requires very sophisticated real-time management of a controlled breach, which in itself could be a risk, unless it is a response that identifies an intrusion and in real time guides the intruder to false findings.

For executives and business managers, small-business owners, industry workers, concerned citizens, and students, the path to finding a road map or starting point to understand the risk landscape as related to insider threat can be difficult. For those with a more informed grasp of the underlying issues of insider threat and who can more accurately assess and mitigate this risk, the quicker the benefits will be realized. As technology continues to evolve in real time, I would illustrate some situational awareness to being normally reliant upon real-time GPS on a smartphone or other linked fitness device with a GPS.

This mobile device is a phone with an advanced operating system that combines the features of a personal computer with sophisticated programs. If an individual was given a paper map, it wouldn't be long before they would likely pull out the smartphone instead, unless they were specifically told and understood all the risks associated with their phones tracking their every geographic position. It's not just that the phones are tracking their positioning, but embedded applications are reporting their location to others. If the risks are not understood, and they often are not, this can create untold risk for an organization. Just ask a teenager where all their friends are right now, and they will likely pull up an app that displays their friends on a global map, even during summer holidays when friends are traveling around the world.

1.1.3 An Insider Threat Employee Monologue

Begin Monologue. I am an unintended insider threat. I am a human being, a person who by virtue of having connections to an organization makes me an insider. You are, too, if you have any inside access to an organization. Despite the fact that I may be a virtuous employee, or even a wicked employee—a MacGyver—I am an unintended insider threat. If I'm pushed too far, I might become vengeful against someone, or even malicious and deliberate against the organization with unintended consequences. I have alliances with friends and family inside the organization, and they will trust me. I might become greedy. Did you know that there are insider threat categories of vengeful employees and malicious employees that are also insider threats, where their actions create unintended consequences along with their original intent? Together, we are all an element of the human risk factor, risk to the collective organization; a risk to the operational mission, business function, and to any program or system where we can open a door. How an organization determines what the risks are, what an acceptable risk is, what is unacceptable, and how to mitigate that risk is an important course of action. This action could be an important deterrent to me—a deterrent to you. Individual awareness, responsibility, and action also mitigate risk; accepting individual responsibility and a greater responsibility for the collective is required of employees, both you and me.

Understanding our human behavior and the potential cascading impacts of our behavior, whether we are aware of our behavior or not, we must however recognize that we both unintentionally and intentionally create vulnerabilities. We meet at the medium, at the crossroads, as a gatekeeper to welcome the outsiders, often with our innocent lenses on. It is not simply an outsider–insider issue. We are on watch, we are the gatekeepers of the crossroads, we guard doors, some visible, some invisible, and often unrecognizable. We must change our behavior. I must change my behavior. We must raise our awareness, recognize our roles, and reduce risk through action to mitigate vulnerability and minimize consequence. You and I, we must develop the workforce to have a core competency in information technology security. We must also monitor ourselves and others for their best interest, and the best interest of the public trust. We must understand risk and try to reduce it. This is what ultimately leads to organizational resilience of unintended insider threat, against you and me. *End monologue.*

1.1.4 The Risk Management Value Proposition

A value proposition for risk management in an organization must be established and shared. As risk management comprehension can be difficult, it is best to begin by understanding that may be defined as *"the process for identifying, analyzing, and communicating risk and accepting, avoiding, transferring, or controlling it to an acceptable level considering associated costs and benefits of any actions taken."*[12] The terms contained in the definition will be contrasted throughout. Within an organization, people have the ability to identify, analyze, and communicate risk even if the decision making about what is accepted, avoided, transferred, or controlled is someone else's final decision-making. Often this is decided after the various associated costs have been calculated into the decision. However, a lot of money could potentially be placed elsewhere for a new opportunity, if people are tuned into risk mitigation techniques. A critical vantage point is needed to shift ideological perspectives and assist the individuals or organizations in all of their connections to become more secure to minimize insider threat, to guide them through organizational assessment and the beneficial mitigation of risk process.

As with most things, money does factor in. Secure technology is also about data integrity and accessibility. It could easily be about life and death. Sometimes people forget about the cascading impacts that real threats can have when risk is not reduced, and there are few resilient measures in place as a plan *b* if plan *a* doesn't work. If you are not familiar with the U.S. Department of Homeland Security National Infrastructure Protection Plan[13] (series), and the various Critical

Infrastructure Sector Specific Plans produced by both the private and public sectors, these documents are worth looking at for clues in your sector about risk management and mitigating risk against physical, cyber, and human risk elements. These plans can be easily found through a search engine, although they do get moved around from time to time. Threats against physical, cyber, and human risk elements must be understood and mitigated for survivability. It is a basic requirement with a significant amount of potentially connected and cascading consequences.

A value proposition is very important for an organization that will be investing dollars into both business process management, and information technology security solutions. Value propositions are not new concepts, and they can apply to entire organizations, or parts of organizations, products, or services. Employees should understand what these value propositions are, and how they relate to the organization, products, and services and their positions. Security can be a challenge because traditionally, organizations have not had to pay for these extra services that need to be acquired. If an old computer still works, it might be a more difficult value proposition to articulate to decision makers why computers must be continuously recapitalized in order to run the latest software with enhanced security features and a new operating system. Indeed, a value proposition is needed inside the organization for cybersecurity protection to an internal customer base of employees, managers, and executives.

Homeland Security Presidential Directive 7 (HSPD-7)[14] established national policy for departments and agencies to identify and prioritize critical infrastructure from terrorist attacks. HSPD-7 identified critical infrastructure sectors in the United States and was essentially put in place to update policies and step up action that was originally intended for terrorist protection under its predecessor Presidential Decision Directive 63. Whereas HSPD-7 took this protection to an entirely superior level under U.S. Department of Homeland Security and in collaboration with both public and private sector partners, both have since been superseded with the issuance of Executive Order 13636 and Presidential Policy Directive (PPD) 21 Critical Infrastructure Security and Resilience. These updates specifically focus on increased cybersecurity, as well as aim for functioning near real-time situational awareness capability for both physical and cyber aspects. The critical infrastructure sector partnership construct has remained fairly solid, as well as the sector specific agencies roles in protection against threats to physical, cyber, and human risk elements. PPD-21 also brought additional focus to security and resilience and described that U.S. policy was to "strengthen the security and resilience of its critical infrastructure against both physical and cyber threats."

These sectors include the communications and the information technology sectors. The information technology sector functions are both virtual and distributed, and include the production of hardware, software, systems, services, and provides the internet collaboratively with the communications sector.[15] The communications sector has evolved over the past 25 years from a voice service provider into a diversity of services where there is significant interoperability between satellite, wireless, and wireline service providers.

Integrity counts here in the long run. While a balance sheet might showcase a particular position to shareholders and executives, the reality is that if an organization's cybersecurity (especially through insider threat identification and prevention) doesn't hold up, this integrity will show through in terms of intrusions and cash outflows to address these breaches. There are simply too many threats that exist beyond the traditional brick and mortar walls of the organization that it's only a matter of time that insider threat will be costly. The opportunity is now to assess and mitigate the risk. Basically, it's time to roll up the sleeves and get to it! Paralysis of actions has led to poor executive decision making, and yes, as we all know doing nothing is a decision; however, doing nothing is not a good option.

Recently I was at a cybersecurity conference where I learned that some government agencies do not have a designated chief information security officer position, or it is at least perceived that they don't within their organization, which is equally as disturbing. In contrast, large organizations in the private sector have increasingly placed a chief information security officer reporting directly to either the chief information officer or the chief executive officer. The chief information security officer is normally responsible for an enterprise perspective, across the organization, to ensure the protection of information and technology assets. Ensuring cybersecurity, or information assurance, is a key role of the chief information security officer. They will provide or guide response capabilities and issue policy to maintain appropriate standards and controls. The role of the chief information security officer should reach every part of an organization to include information privacy, and identity and access management. I would recommend that even mid-size and smaller organizations create this position, in conjunction with the traditional security officer position. Collaboration is needed on both sides. Having this key organizational position is an important value-added consideration. Placement should be equally important depending on the organization where reporting to the chief information officer or the chief executive officer both have merit. Creating a value proposition for having this position is important. Showing the stories of risk in the absence of this position will help to support this establishment. Inherent flexibility and adaptability is very important to your increasingly cyber-savvy workforce.

1.1.5 Mental Models, Storytelling, and Ideological Change

Throughout this book, I use mental models to connect with the reader and to convey meaning for a higher level of conceptualization and hopefully toward an emancipation/ideological shift. Models contribute to understanding through storytelling, and these stories can be shared widely. According to Camp's examination of risk communication, while there is no uniform method for communicating risk, using a mental model could "improve risk communication for computer security."[16] Researchers Blythe and Camp[17] have discussed how mental models can improve education about security, or how to create improved interface with security tools. They also caution that users operate within models that are not necessarily correct and that essentially users may create mental models themselves that manifest the risky behavior. In the absence of clear guidance, employees will likely create practices that may or may not be consistent with realities.

Stories shape organization culture. Stories, especially those that are written or depicted in visual form can continue on well past their original storytellers; even though the original meanings of the stories can change. Unfortunately, not having the right stories to shape a culture is also a concern. Stories often need to have context. In information technology, not enough stories have been developed in an organizational setting. Partly because many of these stories may be guarded due the risk of bad media; errors can make an organization's strength be perceived as vulnerable. However, there is a way to take these lessons learned and create stories to shape the organizational culture often without the absolute specific details. Taking these stories to the abstract level can be successful as well. In terms of insider threat, there is a story that I have heard about this phenomenon. It is that there are two types of organizations: first, those organizations that know they have been a victim of insider threat; and second, those who don't know yet that they have been a victim of insider threat because they do not have a proper monitoring system or insider threat program in place.

There are common foundational risk management practices that have been developed over the last decade, and established more recently, especially at the federal level of government. In order to create a more common understanding and create a risk management culture and philosophy, risk management practices in general have been encouraged, and within the area of cybersecurity encouraged in particular. This doesn't mean to say that all federal agencies have followed advisement diligently; indeed, there have been several significant compromises during the past decade, and this trend doesn't seem to be slowing. Perhaps that is simply a story of "do as I say, not as I do." However, having illusions of protection could easily be the reason why these agencies have allowed such compromises to occur. I chose the word *allow* specifically, because if preventative measures aren't being adequately applied, it is like opening the front door. Sadly, policy might be in place, but absent accountability, continued breaches give the impression that the knowledge isn't there; even when agencies should know better but have not organized nor prioritized for success.

Seemingly, only when media attention has occurred, does a forced resignation or pressure by stakeholders create an opportunity for more aggressive approaches to cybersecurity. It doesn't make for good business airing dirty laundry of what was known, and what could have been mitigated. People can be a challenge to change, and having a rotation of personnel may actually lead to some increase in resilience, if these individuals are willing to shift the process of workflows and consolidations. If employees won't change, it is time to reprogram to a different function, or remove them so that change can occur. On the other hand, valuable information can also be lost in high levels of turnover within an organization.

Mitigation is complicated, even money can't be a quick fix; a greater depth of transformation may need to occur. Computers and systems shouldn't be managed like property because with the layering of new technology on old technology often means that security can't be achieved because *standard configurations* must be modified in order to adapt to the new technology. Standard configuration must be held. When this modification is made then both remote, and in person monitoring of intrusions becomes very difficult. More investment must be made to keep standard configuration up-to-date with recent software, and extremely frequent scanning and full patching of vulnerabilities. Organizations that do not invest in these updates, and allow employees to slack on getting the updates, are at an increased risk. Part of this understanding must be incorporated into the value proposition. In networked organizations, accountability of technology assets is important, as well as the infrastructure that supports them. If an organization does not know what they have, it is difficult for remediation of the issues. Although this sounds almost silly, that organizations don't know what assets they have, this potentially is a high-risk area. Lists of assets must be revalidated through a discovery team. List holders that do not validate their information will soon be questioned about the legitimacy of their knowledge.

Creating stories and mental models that transcend the mumbo-jumbo of technology speak reinforce a cyber-savvy cultural work environment. When a compromise does occur, these compromises should be shared within the organization, especially if the potential has existed that an insider threat helped to facilitate this compromise. Communicating the many computer security risks with employees, so they more fully understand the consequences of their actions and be on the alert for missteps including *social engineering* actions against them is important.

Determining who the strategic communicators are in the organization and examining how they might communicate this risk is relevant. A team may need to be in place to capture these lessons learned, identify remediations, and document subsequent best practices to develop resilience and work toward building a learning and flexible cyber-savvy workforce. These lessons learned should inform the risk landscape. Was this a known threat, or a new threat that led to the increased risk? Was it a threat that was underestimated, or was this an accepted risk, or a risk that was known and not given to the proper organizational leadership to accept the risk. The entire incident now requires additional review and investment to determine impacts to the organizational business model.

I bring discovery to the phenomenon of insider threat and take assessment and risk mitigation to a higher level of understanding, not previously found collected together in the literature. Based on a previous study I conducted, this book takes finding to a higher level of practitioner application and shares the knowledge well beyond the academic setting.

While theory is important, it is also time for leaders to learn more about how to articulate a value proposition for cybersecurity, identify their organizational assets, what their vulnerabilities are related to consequences, and what risk management decisions should be considered, and to make potential policy changes. In practicality, a more tactical focus will include managing vulnerabilities and applying countermeasures. Understanding the relationship to the criticality of the organization in particular, will guide the reader to a greater depth of understanding, and creating action-oriented options.

Sometimes ideological changes have to be told in the form of stories. One spring day in the year 2001, after attending an ASPA conference sponsored by Rutgers University–Newark Campus in New Jersey, I looked toward the New York skyline. I was driving, it was evening, and it looked very beautiful from afar, the city lights twinkling like stars. I saw the picturesque Twin Towers, which were the signature structure of the World Trade Center as part of the skyline. I thought to myself, I should stop and take a picture, long before smartphone technology was in full force. But I decided I would get the picture on my next trip and even thought to myself *the skyline will be there next time.* Then shortly thereafter the terrorist attacks of September 11, 2001 (9/11) occurred, and the skyline was drastically not the same. The impossible now seemed possible, no matter how permanent something might be perceived, and how limited I might have been in my thinking at that time, 9/11 created an ideological shift in the realm of possibility for many people.

I learned much from Dr. Horowitz, a sociology professor in my undergraduate studies. He used to ask his students, "How do we know that each day the sun will rise?" He would go on to explain that because *it always had before* was a limited assertion, because one day *it just might not* rise; this could be attributed to a larger pattern, that we just haven't observed, or come to know yet. It is a theory until we gain additional data that we can put together into a higher level of understanding of the environment.

The 9/11 terrorist attacks on U.S. soil, when four hijacked planes crashed in New York, Virginia, and Pennsylvania, changed the course of global history, including the ideological outlook of many nations including the United States. The findings from this day, which included the tragic loss of almost 3,000 people who lost their lives, is well documented in the *9/11 Commission Report*.[18] The impossible became the possible, and the U.S. government's failure of imagination was called into play. Not just imagination, because a small plane accidentally or intentionally hitting the Twin Towers was within the realm of imagination already, but that this action would be taken to another level with a commercial airliner, and that this would have such an unimaginable consequence. The 9/11 Commission learned of the enemy who was *sophisticated, patient, disciplined, and lethal*; one could expect that this type of adversary now exists with a higher level of technological capability than over 15 years ago. A lesson learned showed how unprepared several agencies were, and in the face of increasing threats where *policies, plans, and practices to deter or defeat* were not adjusted. Where not all risk can be eliminated, organizations should not allow virtual doors or holes in the fences to allow the external threat in. Employees may not even realize how much risk they are creating within the organization.

In spring of 1999, I was on floor 107 of the World Trade Center, in the Windows on the World, guided by a U.S. Coast Guard Public Affairs Reserve Officer, before I went to a Manhattan planning meeting for a future tall ships event. I had never been in a building so high, and looking down all the bridges looked so small, like toys. I have since come to appreciate this brief moment, this vantage point, on an entirely different level. It was explained to me by my guide about the people who worked there regularly, had worked there for decades. The sun would not come up for 79 career restaurant employees, nor the elevator operator, nor their guests, following the terrorist attacks of 9/11.[19] When I reflect on critical thinking and ideology, I think about these people because I met several of them on my journey. They represent to me how threat was not properly assessed or mitigated, and this created the ultimate consequence, devastation of livelihood and an iconic business, and death of employees. Above all, this illustrated to me an extreme ideological shift that the United States would come to experience. Although this is on the more extreme spectrum of consequences, it illustrates our ever-changing landscape of risk in the United States and risk mitigation considerations for organizations.

Just because a security breach cannot be visually seen doesn't mean it has not, or will not, soon occur. The risk landscape may be captured in a moment, but it has the potential to be ever changing. Insider threat is a high organizational risk that must be mitigated with a deliberate approach and methodology. Every organization needs to ensure they truly understand the concept of insider threat and obtain a clear value proposition. The span of what insider threat is, based on my research, shows that it is significantly broader than what much of the existing literature describes. Through stories, organizations can learn more about their insider threat picture as well as create opportunities through storytelling that will shape ideological change.

Endnotes

1. Loch, E. D., Carr, H. H., & Warkentin, M. E. (1992). Threats to information systems: Today's reality, yesterday's understanding. *MIS Quarterly*, 15(2), 173–186. Retrieved from http://www.misq.org/.
2. Warkentin, M. & Willison, R. (2009). Behavioral and policy issues in information systems security; the insider threat. *European Journal of Information Systems*, 18, 101–105. doi:10.1057/ejis.2009.12.
3. Federal Emergency Management Agency. Retrieved from www.fema.gov.
4. Information Technology Sector-Specific Plan; an Annex to the National Infrastructure Protection Plan, U.S. Department of Homeland Security, 2010.
5. Ibid.
6. Andrew Feenberg, a Canada Research Chair in Philosophy of Technology. CV. 2016. Retrieved from http://www.sfu.ca/~andrewf/.
7. United States Computer Emergency Readiness Team. 2015. Retrieved from www.us-cert.gov.
8. National Coordination Office for Space-Based Positioning, Navigation, and Timing. Official U.S. government information about the Global Positioning Systems (GPS) and related topics. GPS.gov. 2016. Retrieved from http://www.gps.gov/spectrum/jamming/.

9. Hacker Disables More Than 100 Cars Remotely by Poulsen, K. *Wired.* March 17, 2010. Retrieved from http://www.wired.com/2010/03/hacker-bricks-cars/.

10. Archuleta out at OPM by Zach Noble, *FCW: The Business of Federal Technology.* July 10, 2015. Retrieved from https://fcw.com/articles/2015/07/10/archuleta-out-at-opm.aspx.

11. Inside the OPM Hack, the Cyberattack That Shocked the U.S. Government by Brendan, I. Koerner. *Wired.* October 23, 2016. Retrieved from https://www.wired.com/2016/10/inside-cyberattack-shocked-us-government/.

12. U.S. Department of Homeland Security. DHS Risk Lexicon, 2010 edition.

13. National Infrastructure Protection Plan, U.S. Department of Homeland Security, 2006, 2009, 2013.

14. Homeland Security Presidential Directive 7: Critical Infrastructure Identification, Prioritization, and Protection. December 17, 2003. Retrieved from www.dhs.gov.

15. Communications and Information Technology Sector Snapshot, series. U.S. Department of Homeland Security. 2015. Retrieved from www.dhs.gov.

16. Camp, L. J. (2009). Mental models of privacy and security. *IEEE Technology and Society Magazine*, 28(3), 37–48. doi:10.1109/MTS.2009.0=934142.

17. Blythe, J. & Camp, J. L. (2012). Implementing mental models. *Security and Privacy Workshops, 2012 IEEE Symposium*, pp. 80–90. doi:10.1109/SPW.2012.31.

18. The 9/11 Commission Report, Official Government Edition. U.S. Government Printing Office. Retrieved from www.gpo.gov.

19. Windows of the World, New York's Sky-High Restaurant, by Morabito, G. *New York Eater.* September 11, 2013. Retrieved from http://ny.eater.com/2013/9/11/6547477/windows-on-the-world-new-yorks-sky-high-restaurant.

2

INSIDER CYBERSECURITY THREATS TO ORGANIZATIONS

2.1 Introduction

Insider threat is a human–computer threat that is often highly misunderstood because of the well-publicized and documented classic cases of insider threat by malicious insiders. For example, early in 2010, shortly after becoming an analyst, Bradley Manning as a U.S. Army Intelligence Analyst with a Top Secret/Sensitive Compartmented Information Clearance started, unbeknownst to the U.S. government, leaking volumes of classified government and military documents to an open source forum located in Sweden called WikiLeaks. In simple terms, WikiLeaks serves as the middleman for leaking various types of information to the press. It is estimated that three-quarters of a million pages of classified documents were released by Manning. Not surprisingly, Manning was later arrested in May of 2010, and by 2013, he was sentenced to 35 years in prison after conviction.[1]

Surprisingly, this is not the end of the story of Manning who received early release from U.S. President Obama in January 2017. This release came shortly before his presidency came to an end and was a commuted sentence from 35 to 7 years, and remains under great controversy. Bradley Manning, during the times of his malicious activity, was also experiencing gender dysphoria and later became Chelsea Manning. There have been a lot of facts and speculations presented about the life and times of Manning. There is one story that has not received as much press, and it is a fascinating article as told by Jay Huwieler,[2] a boot camp classmate of Bradley Manning, who describes Manning as someone who quit and even sabotaged his team by passing incorrect information, bragging about breaking the rules about acquiring prohibited candy, and giving up; last seen the company thought Manning had washed out for failure to adapt, but he was later recycled back in. Notably, Huwieler asserts that when the going got tough, Manning was there to say "I can't" and did not appear to learn from his mistakes, nor connect with fellow recruits who were working as a team. From a security standpoint, "Manning altered not only the way we think about information security, authentication, and confidentiality, but also the grave damage posed by the insider threat."

Although transcripts show Manning as both vengeful and malicious, his earlier behavior could be attributed to someone who was wicked and vengeful. The cascading consequences of Manning's unauthorized release of classified information is also extensive, and although much is known about the damage, the full extent of this damage is yet to be quantified.

It is fairly clear to the importance of understanding insider threat that these overtly malicious cases must be analyzed because malicious insider attacks result in a very high level of consequence, including likely at the national security level. However, it should also not be at the expense of conducting more internal in-depth analysis of insider threat, unmaliciously in nature to include the virtuous, wicked, and vengeful. These examinations should occur together, a gestalt leading to the mitigation of this risk; the process to identify, analyze, and communicate risk, to avoid it, transfer it, and control it to an acceptable level.

Indeed, if a malicious mental model of insider threat is used exclusively without a greater breadth of focus on the risk landscape, then this limited way of thinking will increase organizational risk. Organizational understanding must focus on not just the technological factors, not just on the malicious actors, but also on a much greater breadth of human factors. As technology changes, such as with mobile technology, some of these human factors of behavior will change, although several typologies of behavior are likely to remain if left unchecked or if not continually assessed and mitigated. An organization should not have a stagnant insider threat program, but should be an ongoing assessment of emerging human factors including virtuous, wicked, vengeful, and malicious.

There is generally less media sensation when a digital forensic investigation reveals that an intrusion occurred because someone with an increased level of administrative privileges simply walked away to get coffee and unwittingly left their computer terminal open. We are less likely to hear about these cases nationally in the news even if these human behaviors resulted in compromise.

The fundamental question for this chapter: "What are the insider threats to organizations?" First, I provide a narrative response that will directly answer the question, then I provide a listing of categories displayed in Table 2.1; these categories are listed for readability in terms of Core Categories as well as their cascading sub-categories which follow. Last, toward the end of the chapter, I enter into a more comprehensive dialogue about these findings. Throughout the discussion, practical applications, mental models, and best practices are called out. Specifically the categories may be used by an organization to identify controls that they should use to mitigate the risk element. A staffing cycle to minimize insider threat is also outlined for consideration. Doctrine related to risk management is strongly suggested along with an assessment worksheet that is based on implementation related to cybersecurity and privacy.

What are the insider threats to organizations? The answers follow.

2.1.1 *The Narrative Response*

- Any person or artificial intelligence that has access to an organization, by virtue of insider status, could create virtual or physical access to organizational humans, systems, or networks' virtual or physical locations to create an insider cybersecurity threat including tangible loss to organization vis-à-vis:
  - An unintended security threat that could be introduced by an action, or inaction by
    1. A well-intended virtuous employee with an unintended outcome; or,
    2. A wicked employee (not vengeful or malicious) with an intended purpose, but potentially an unintended outcome; or,

- An intended security threat that could be introduced by an action, or inaction by
  1. A vengeful disgruntled employee with an intended outcome, however an unintended, unplanned outcome could still occur; or,
  2. A deliberate and intended malicious targeted action or inaction that may have been preplanned, or happenstance, and may result in an intended, or unintended outcome.
  - Note that an understanding of the term *employee* should be expanded to include a surrogate employee (temporary, volunteer) or a third party (such as contractor, service provider, vendor, or inside user of a product or service).
- Insider cybersecurity threats to organizations also include organizational supporting mechanisms. For example: policy; architectural enterprise structure; mission support capability including senior management communications; logistics, financial, and contractual support; information sharing; and, policing activity. The element of time as well as unguarded access, are also contributing risk factors of insider cybersecurity threats to organization.
- The entry point of the insider threat occurs at a convergence point, the crossroads at the organizational medium. A boundary that may be considered the threshold for access.

2.1.2 The Categorical Response

Now that the narrative has been presented, I will list the categorical results that have supported this narrative. These categorical results may be used in terms of an assessment in order to mitigate risk and to initially identify the organizational responsibility and known controls. Please keep in mind that these are insider threats to organization and are not representative of any one particular organization, nor apply to all organizations; however, they should be considered by all organizations at various levels of size. Even at an individual level some of these categories could apply; but the development of the extensive list was principally centered on the organization or business environment.

If you have not have considered these threats, or do not have the Core Categories assigned to an individual responsible or have not assigned controls in your organization to mitigate these threats, then your risk is likely quite high. The good news is that you can learn from this material and apply mitigating controls within your organization. The lead/control I have written in the far-right column in Table 2.1 is an example of what you might create within your organization. This control can vary depending on regulatory or business standards and practices. For the federal government, they are often guided by the National Institute of Standards and Technology (NIST) Standards for Information Technology. The lead could be the department of an organization, such as the human resources management department, or the financial department, each in collaboration with the information department or traditional (physical) security services department. This variation will depend on the current organizational structure; however, keep in mind that after reviewing this book and conducting an assessment, there is a good possibility that you will make changes that will restructure some responsibilities in order to enhance internal security and drive mitigation of risks to a more acceptable level.

Collaboration is very important between various security departments within an organization. Unfortunately traditional structures have polarized security professionals and as a result, increased risks inside many organizations. For each Insider Core Category, you will want to ensure that a lead security professional is assigned. It could include lead positions such as chief information officer or chief operating officer, for example, but I have listed other areas for consideration. A testing program should be implemented to assess the levels of risks which will vary depending on the associated category. For example, developing and implementing a social engineering testing program, and/or creating a red team/blue team for testing scenarios along with responses to those situations is a way to analyze and communicate risk. Additionally, as an organization, you will want to ensure that you have properly planned for your response to a given event or breach, and determining who might have a lead in this response area will be important.

Table 2.1   Insider Cyber Threats to Organization

CATEGORY	CORE CATEGORY = C, OR SUB-CATEGORY = S	LEAD, CO-LEAD, AND CONTROL
Core	**A. Any Human Employee, Surrogate Employee, or Third Party Who Could Have Virtual or Physical Access to Networks or Systems**	**Assign an organization lead; establish controls, risk communications, traditional security, human resources, acquisitions, and cybersecurity**
S	Employee.	
S	Contractor.	
S	Volunteer.	
S	Customer.	
S	Customer of customers (tertiary).	
S	Temporary or transient workers.	
S	Those who are detailed to or from a different location.	
S	Initial physical site setup for workers/or people with access to site.	
S	Malicious attacker/hacker that targets, or is the neighborhood.	
S	Artificial intelligence.	
S	Privileged user.	
S	Administrative with access.	
Core	**B. People Engaging in Manifest or Latent Risky Behavior (Vulnerability)**	**Assign an organization lead; establish controls, risk communications, traditional security, training, human resources, and cybersecurity**
S	Good/virtuous employees trying to get the job done to meet deadlines (transporter, revealer, discarder).	
S	Wicked employees.	
S	Unmonitored or non-compliant privileged user.	
S	Disgruntled employee(s).	
S	Routine employee(s).	
S	Lazy employees.	
S	Rushed employees.	
S	Inexperienced employees.	
S	Untrained employees.	
S	Complacency of user.	
S	Under-resourced security personnel.	
S	Complacency of security personnel.	
S	Poor IT security hygiene of employee.	

(Continued)

Table 2.1 (*Continued*)   Insider Cyber Threats to Organization

CATEGORY	CORE CATEGORY = C, OR SUB-CATEGORY = S	LEAD, CO-LEAD, AND CONTROL
S	Persons seeking unauthorized gain.	
S	People with malicious intent/attacks.	
S	Employees who lose things.	
S	Employees who are tricked.	
S	Recruited insider.	
S	Employees who reveal information.	
S	Innovative MacGyver, employee(s) creating a work-around.	
S	Employees finding extra privileges and using them.	
S	Workers lacking and not maintaining ongoing situational awareness.	
S	Not using the correct disposal process for media.	
S	Printing work material on home computer printers.	
S	Lack of auditing performance.	
S	Limited understanding of threat and risk.	
S	Users having too much access.	
S	Basic users having root access.	
S	Privileged users with too much access.	
S	Privileged user not being audited.	
S	Managers not ensuring role-based access.	
S	Security personnel not locking down systems.	
S	Not budgeting enough money for IT security.	
S	Ignoring guidelines.	
S	Ignoring policy.	
S	Not updating guidelines and policy.	
S	Not providing operational users with right tools.	
S	Not enforcing.	
S	Employees who throw out data.	
S	Employees who tolerate others' poor IT security hygiene.	
S	Employees who leave things unattended.	
S	Employees who allow others to obtain information not authorized.	
S	Employees who collect information without protecting it.	
S	Employees who engage in activities to produce unauthorized gain.	

(*Continued*)

Table 2.1 (*Continued*) Insider Cyber Threats to Organization

CATEGORY	CORE CATEGORY = C, OR SUB-CATEGORY = S	LEAD, CO-LEAD, AND CONTROL
S	Not having proper security processes/ mechanisms to refer alerts or concerns of employees.	
S	Not prioritizing enough money for IT security.	
S	Not communicating security risks and mitigations with employees.	
S	Sending to unverified source.	
S	Revealing information that has unknown sensitivity.	
S	Not having or following password security guidelines.	
S	A reveal of almost anything in the organization.	
S	Reveal of the organizational structure and function.	
S	Giving out passwords/divulging passwords.	
S	Privileged users playing around.	
S	Privileged users creating false accounts to violate policy.	
S	Privileged users with malicious intent.	
S	Gathering info over time, obtains big picture for gain/personal use.	
S	Persons gaining unauthorized access.	
S	People giving out privileged information.	
S	Individuals not protecting personally identifiable info of self/family.	
S	Not applying the proper permissions.	
S	Unlocking folders to show people.	
S	People not properly vetted or missed info in vetting process.	
S	Incorrectly transmitting out of organization (zip/password protect).	
Core	**C. Tangible Loss. A consequence that transcends personnel, physical, and IT systems security extending to individuals, organizations, customers, and/or consumers. Tangible loss may be perceived, specifically measured, or appraised**	**Assign an organization lead; establish controls, risk communications, traditional security, human resources, financial managers, and cybersecurity**
S	Loss of physical assets.	

(*Continued*)

Table 2.1 (*Continued*) Insider Cyber Threats to Organization

CATEGORY	CORE CATEGORY = C, OR SUB-CATEGORY = S	LEAD, CO-LEAD, AND CONTROL
S	Loss of electronic data (virtual storage/ physical storage).	
S	Enterprise system shutdown (physical systems can't connect to virtual).	
S	Loss of financial data.	
S	Operational mission compromise.	
S	Loss of employee to productivity.	
S	Loss of employee to death.	
S	Loss of employee due to lack of respect, and faith in organization.	
S	Loss of employee to termination.	
S	Manifested legal action, monetary cost.	
S	Loss of protected knowledge.	
S	Cascading tangible impacts.	
S	Breaking evidence chains.	
S	Release of security information of significance.	
S	Physical security breach.	
S	Gaining access to virtual via physical infrastructure accessibility (lock-a-ways).	
S	Gaining access to virtual through human social engineering.	
S	Traditional spy gaining access through physical to gain to virtual (vice versa).	
S	A disclosure of information, including need-to-know disclosure.	
S	A denial of service.	
S	As mitigation disrupting user or shutting down system without checking on kinetic impact to operations.	
S	Cost of forensic investigation.	
S	Loss of capability due to restrictions imposed.	
S	Loss of public trust or reputation.	
Core	**D. Sans, Unknown, or Out-of-Date Policy**	**Assign an organization lead; establish controls, risk communications, traditional security, human resources, cybersecurity, and other consolidated policy lead**
S	Outdated or nonexistent IT security policy.	
S	Policy not promulgated.	

(*Continued*)

Table 2.1 (*Continued*)   Insider Cyber Threats to Organization

CATEGORY	CORE CATEGORY = C, OR SUB-CATEGORY = S	LEAD, CO-LEAD, AND CONTROL
S	Policy not coordinated well, a need for top down and bottom up.	
S	Not managing customer expectations, changing rules midway without communications or collaboration.	
S	Policy not accessible to users and managers.	
S	Hit or miss information sharing.	
Core	**E. Architectural, Information Technology Enterprise System Risk**	**Assign an organization lead; establish controls, risk communications, traditional security, system engineers, and cybersecurity**
S	New technology on old system structure.	
S	Open access to particular parts of system.	
S	Operational systems on administrative systems.	
S	Enterprise level openings.	
S	Unsecure folders, unsecure portals, unencrypted backups.	
S	Systemic safeguards not in place.	
S	Bypassing through technology work-around that goes initially undetected.	
S	Devices that are connected.	
S	Change made on enterprise or centralized help desk level, without understanding impacts at lower level.	
S	Unauthorized computers on network.	
Core	**F. Inadequate Operational Mission Support Capability**	**Assign an organization lead and establish controls; risk communications, traditional security, human resources, financial managers, acquisitions, and cybersecurity**
S	Inadequate tools, leaving roadblocks for operators to do their mission within policy and guidelines.	
S	Closing alerts/warnings (tickets) too early before follow-through.	
S	Making fixes without seeking operational impact of fixes vs. security risk.	
S	Administrative system used as an operational system platform.	

(*Continued*)

Table 2.1 (*Continued*)   Insider Cyber Threats to Organization

CATEGORY	CORE CATEGORY = C, OR SUB-CATEGORY = S	LEAD, CO-LEAD, AND CONTROL
S	Gaps between traditional/physical security and information technology security during incident response; information assurance.	
S	Lack of communications from senior management on threats, risk, mitigation.	
S	Lack of collaboration from senior organizational managers on mitigation actions and understanding kinetic impact on operations.	
S	Need understanding at lower classification level of threat.	
S	Elitism, not developing trust.	
S	Lack of communication, loss of chain-of command.	
Core	**G. Logistic, Financial, and/or Contractual Support Inadequacy or Compromise**	**Assign an organization lead and establish controls; risk communications, traditional security, human resources, financial manager, acquisitions expert, and cybersecurity**
S	Stealing information related to contracts and acquisitions.	
S	Blackmail.	
S	Personally identifiable information theft.	
S	Lack of money to support security control programs/systems.	
S	Unsupported equipment, including required equipment or standards not supported.	
S	Out-of-date equipment, no communications before shutoff.	
S	Lack of memorandums of understanding, memorandums of agreement, or service-level agreements.	
Core	**H. Information Mismanagement**	**Assign organization lead and establish controls; risk communications, traditional security, human resources, privacy, and cybersecurity**
S	Databases of people not protected.	
S	Database of people's responsibilities revealed unnecessarily.	
S	Storing personally identifiable information incorrectly.	

(*Continued*)

Table 2.1 (*Continued*)   Insider Cyber Threats to Organization

CATEGORY	CORE CATEGORY = C, OR SUB-CATEGORY = S	LEAD, CO-LEAD, AND CONTROL
S	Using buddy system and not verifying authority.	
S	Knowing repeated problems; needed oversight of repeated problems.	
S	Sharing knowledge w/ inner circle, spouses, and friends with information that shouldn't be shared.	
Core	**I. Policing**	**Assign organization lead and establish controls; risk communications, traditional security, human resources, privacy, and cybersecurity**
S	Information assurance not keeping up with technology needs.	
S	Users formally acknowledging acceptance of risk on behalf of organization, not understanding scope of threat(s).	
S	Being reactive, resulting in restrictions being imposed limiting capability.	
S	Not ensuring proper check-in and check-out of personnel.	
S	Internal audit controls.	
Core	**J. Time Threats**	**Assign organization lead and establish controls; risk communications, traditional security, human resources, privacy, and cybersecurity**
S	Time of year, for example, holidays; more people shopping.	
S	A particular event-time.	
S	News or viral media that creates opportunity for trickery.	
S	Data collection over time, potential for time-delayed impact.	
S	Time between identified compromise and response that coordinates together human resource physical action and technological security action.	

2.1.3 Assessing Risk

This table has provided a lot of categorical results to think about in terms of insider threat at large. It may, and should, be used as a practical check sheet to determine how these results apply to your organization and are being considered within your organization. Take note in particular on who is currently responsible for them, if anyone. It is a lot of information to cover, whereas much of this knowledge has more recently been compiled, some areas may be less familiar to you. Use the right column to identify who should have lead and if accountability exists or if it is a gap area.

Depending on your organization's structure it may call to attention gaps in security coverage. Once it has been determined which group has ownership, a controls chart can be developed. For those items that are not covered, a road map can be developed to further bridge the mitigation of risk given your identified vulnerabilities.

2.1.4 Risk Scoring

Each category can also be given a risk score of high, medium, and low risk with or without the controls currently in place for comparative purposes. It is a good idea to understand the risk landscape and what your baseline picture is with no controls in place. Essentially, so that activities can be measured from the baseline of maximum risk if nothing is controlled. Then you can account for the risk picture which includes the efforts already in place, to see expenses and results related to risk mitigation activities. This can also greatly assist in budget justifications when explaining to resource boards or higher authorities, hi-level prioritization for funding considerations. When calculating risk, sometimes there has to be an acceptable level related to associated costs, and benefits of actions. An example of this might be protecting against nuclear threat. Yes, the threat exists, and the consequences are high, especially with an intense pulse of electromagnetic radiation.[3] However, if an investment was only made in protecting employees from a nuclear attack, there wouldn't be much of a budget left to protect the organization against more likely scenarios such as individuals operating on computer systems without proper authentication. At a minimum, investing in a minimum two-factor authentication, and ideally multi-factor authentication for both employee access to the network and the cloud, as well as multi-factor authentication servers and other resources would be wise. Money might be better invested in exploring these security solutions. Without security assurance, trusted reputations quickly dissolve, and there is business loss.

Please note that not all of the categories above may apply to you, but they should be considered in your insider threat assessment and mitigation of risks. If you have identified more, then add them. If you already have existing checkoff sheets, cross-check them for insider threat vulnerabilities that you might have missed with the various leads as suggested.

2.1.5 Deeper Dive into Insider Cybersecurity Threats to Organization

So now that I have addressed the answer to this fundamental question and provided an initial way forward for assessment (there is more to come), I will take a deeper dive and describe the insider cybersecurity threats to organizations with greater specificity and practical application so that as you go through the categories you are able to understand the applications. A quick summary of what has been identified thus far.

Restating for emphasis, the following 10 emergent themes are part of, and/or factors of insider threat:

- Organizational access and connections, including the recognition of a medium (similar to a threshold)
- Human behavior
- Tangible loss
- Policy gaps
- Enterprise system risk
- Operational support needs
- Finance and logistic challenges
- Information mismanagement
- Policing
- Time as a threat consideration

Whereas these emergent themes may not be representative of all organizations, they certainly demonstrate the breadth of insider threat to organizations that should be considered. The first emergent theme was that of organizational access and connections, entry points that were not always perceived as being a well-known vulnerability. Next was that of risky human behavior, there were a lot of different types identified; for example, employees who easily lose things and those who are tricked, ultimately leading to tangible types of loss including information and capability.

Although policy is not always something that initially comes to mind with information technology specialists, the identified contribution of policy, and related gaps, is often spoken about and has become increasingly important. Emerging themes of enterprise system risk challenges are often discussed in terms of connections and openings, and understanding how sophisticated enterprise systems are shared/integrated. Organizational access and the specific connection(s) emphasis were especially important as a basic fundamental. Who is considered an insider is expanded somewhat by these categories.

Inadequate support often centered on support that was intended to help could create additional problems if coupled with poor communications. This is part of the risk management picture. Finance and logistic challenges and concerns are fairly consistent themes along with challenges in information mismanagement and policing for information assurance especially where growth in technology continues. The concept of time is less known in the literature as related to information technology security, but has been elevated as an emergent theme. The discovery of an insider and outsider crossroads convergence phenomenon redefined the insider threat by introducing an in-between medium as an area for which unintended insider threat, especially human behavior, may be exploited.

2.2 Organizational Access and Connections

I am intrigued by this topic of insider cybersecurity threats to organization because little research had been done to understand—more holistically—insider threat, and even more so, unintended insider threat, prior to my study on the topic. A lot more focus on the exterior perimeter of physical security and even cybersecurity defense had been made to try and keep the bad guys out of an organization, essentially the malicious intruders or actors.

There are documented efforts to detect the disguised malicious insider who might have worked in the organizational midst, in a classic spy or espionage scenario, if you will. Studies have been designed to focus on behavior that is not considered consistent with common practice of an individual; the anomaly which makes the malicious actor stand out, especially when that human is an active threat and intentionally interfering with decision-making processes through manipulation of perception.[4]

An insider threat that perhaps was intentionally interfering with denial of service or was simply collecting data to relay to an external source; essentially intelligence gathering that includes institutional information from the inside as well as information gathering from public sources. Industrial espionage is understood to mean spying that is a *State*-sponsored actor, for example, the Republic of China spying on the United States through the positioning of a malicious employee in a U.S. agency. There have been several case study examples of this type of espionage throughout U.S. history.

Through recent negotiations, a spy exchange was agreed upon in December of 2014 and highlights the issue of this ongoing threat. In a reversal of long-established U.S. foreign policy with Cuba, the United States traded the release of three Cuban spies for that of a U.S. intelligence asset and a humanitarian release of a USAID subcontractor who the United States claims was wrongfully imprisoned.[5] In December of 2014, President Barack Obama spoke with Fidel Castro via telephone; on the same day the press secretary engaged the public and provided the president's fact sheet charting a new course with Cuba.[6]

Access to organizations is created by humans and exploited through technology. Humans simply open the doors, despite the motivation behind their actions, the results end up being the same. Doors are open. It has become very clear that the discipline of information technology security has continued to evolve in response to the continuous increased threat and actual level of successful compromise.

The release of millions of the U.S. Office of Personnel Management (OPM) files with very sensitive personally identifiable information, also known as PII, was previously discussed. I categorize this as a negligent release, because the prevention of this breach was more easily controlled than the agency wanted to admit. With the congressional attention and testimony, I winced at the uninformed responses of those being called to testify for OPM, simply denying again and again a clear accountability. I spoke to a U.S. Congressman in a non-attribution forum who said to me, "Why didn't they just apologize? I never heard them say 'that was my fault."

Furthermore, a July 2015 memorandum from the OPM's Office of the Inspector General (OIG) summarizing several serious concerns called out OPM's chief information officer who they believed provided inaccurate and misleading information which was subsequently repeated at congressional hearings by the now former OPM director Katherine Archuleta.[7] The OIG had the responsibility to conduct independent and objective oversight of agency operations, but this was not conducted in a timely manner, and ultimately as access was compromised, information was placed in the wrong hands.

The inspector general went on to claim that they were not informed of the first data breach, nor were they informed of a major new initiative made by the chief information officer to overhaul the agency's information technology environment until over a year after these technology investment efforts had begun. The inspector general also claimed that they were tactically delayed in audits even though compromises had occurred, where they were told they could not interfere with remediation efforts by OPM's chief information officer because of similar reviews being conducted by the U.S. Department of Homeland Security. Essentially, the OIG had not been properly informed, and this lack of communication limited the ability for interagency coordination with law enforcement as well as hampered their ability to conduct audit oversight.

Organizational access and connections need to be known. Authorized access and connections still need to be monitored with audit controls in place, including being able to isolate compromises. Sadly, the lack of proper response has likely showcased to the world the existing risk landscape of insider threat protection ineffectiveness and future opportunities for hackers to find that open door. A door for which at this point appears to be a revolving door that is not locked.

During a second breach, auditors from OPM's OIG were surprisingly excluded from meetings that OPM's chief information officer had with the Federal Bureau of Investigation and DHS's U.S. Computer Readiness Team (US-CERT)—where the inspector general was told their presence would interfere with the FBI and US-CERT's work. The OIG did not release for public consumption the very specific details attached to the memorandum which described with greater specificity the misleading information asserted to have been provided by the chief information officer. Interestingly enough, at the time of the breach, the inspector general, who had served since 1990, was the longest-standing inspector general in federal government. Yet, the knowledge of what really was going on at the agency was not identified.

The reality is that the times have changed, and our society has rapidly transformed into a society of digital culture, continuously and progressively since the early 1990s. Organizations can no longer simply deny responsibility, but must endeavor to create a risk informed culture that reduces risk through a variety of means, all the while aware of the greater threat picture.

Yes, there are gaps in the workforce competency across various sizes of organizations. There remains a lack of cybersecurity experts, but this doesn't mean that the competency can't be grown to meet the needs of the future workforce. However, to think that newly trained information specialists will have the experience to thwart these attacks is unrealistic. It takes time, and relevant experience, to develop an adequate skill set in this highly complex playing field. OPM, if anyone, who is in the business of human resource management, should have seen this coming. In fact, in 2009 and the years since, the Executive Office of the President of the United States has issued a comprehensive national cybersecurity initiative that should have helped to prepare the agency in defending against immediate threats, full spectrum, and for the future. OPM should have been on the cutting edge to inform other agencies of how to attract, hire, and inherently train a cyber-savvy workforce. Yet they failed miserably. This leaves us with a nagging question on the role of accountability and compelling compliance. Quite frankly, not enough people in OPM were fired. The information acquired could negatively impact millions and lead to greater consequences that we just don't know about yet.

The irony of this compromise has been overshadowed because of the potential impact of the massive data loss. The irony exists because

OPM should have been helping to develop and establish the criteria for a cyber-savvy workforce that would propel the United States as a world leader well into the future. Failures like this have international impacts.

When Hurricane Katrina made landfall in the United States, over-all, the response was less than ideal. This has been well documented and is widely known. As time continues to march onward, readers may not be as familiar with Hurricane Katrina which struck Florida and the Gulf Coast states including Louisiana at the end of August 2005; there were many lessons learned from this tragic disaster response. This all-hazard event caused a national shift in the resiliency of the nation, no matter what had actually caused the disruption. Man-made or all hazards; much focus had been on organizing the Department of Homeland Security and attempting to thwart terrorist attacks in a post–9/11 environment. Rightfully so, but responsibility and focus needed to span further toward a greater breadth of mission areas. If a chief executive officer has not installed the right people to lead, or is not prioritizing multiple missions, or crosscutting functions such as cybersecurity, there will be problems when a crisis emerges. How critical those problems will become, will depend on very specific advanced planning that will assess potential threats and mitigate against risk.

Shortly after Hurricane Katrina made landfall, I served as a U.S. delegate for the White House to the International Maritime Organization under the then-President G.W. Bush administration representing the United States from the Coast Guard. It was a very difficult time for the international community to understand why the United States was not able to protect more people from the initial impact by means of evacuation, as well as the aftermath that ensued. Indeed, resiliency was not optimal, and the media response showcased extreme looting, terrible life-threatening conditions, and a fallen city government response. U.S. failures were harshly judged internationally; with the ideology that if the United States, as a *superpower*, was not able to protect their own communities, then how could the United States legitimately tell other countries what to do. Notably, Cuban dictator Fidel Castro offered immediate and significant assistance to the United States offering over 1,500 doctors and medical supplies, but the United States failed to accept this offer.[8] News media reports from around the globe showcased the dire conditions around the world, from the ground perspective.

I received a telephone message at work from my father, since deceased, who at the time was living in Montreal, Quebec, Canada. We were a holiday-cards-only family, and he had never called me at work before, but was pleading in desperation for the United States to do something for the people at the Superdome where conditions had deteriorated. Yes, the world was judging the United States; we were a failure, judgment was made. Emergency response to evacuate people was hampered because of badly coordinated logistics, while news reporters spoke that they were easily able to drive in and report on the horrid conditions. Soon after Hurricane Katrina had actually made landfall, I saw the former director of the U.S. Federal Management Agency (FEMA) Michael Brown giving a press interview with a positive spin, and thought to myself "Oh no, it's too soon to know the impact, it hasn't even been assessed; didn't his people tell him what he needs to do?" The reorganization of multiple agencies into the Department of Homeland Security was quickly showing its toll in emergency response. Despite this low moment, the U.S. Coast Guard rescued 30,000 people and Vice Admiral Thad Allen became the principal federal official, and needed voice of authority, calm, and reason to direct and aid response efforts.

Since that time, additional congressional action has taken place. Enhancements and clarifications of mission, functions, and authorities were defined for FEMA within the Department of Homeland Security. Because FEMA was reorganized under the Homeland Security Act of 2002, it was argued that authorities had eroded and were misplaced. Therefore, most preexisting responsibilities were reestablished under the Post-Katrina Emergency Management Reform Act of 2006,[9] including additional responsibilities and authorities to the lead administrator to ensure first responder effectiveness. Accountability is often felt at the top of organizations, as it should be, as well as throughout the organization. There are many who influence decision makers, selecting the correct sphere of influence can be a challenge.

There are more physical, cyber, and human connections than you are likely to realize in your organization; however, you are also likely smart enough to keep an open mind to explore what those access and connection points are today, or could become tomorrow. This is a good place to assess where those access points are and a beginning point to shift your ideology and approaches. The information presented likely has you thinking about next steps in your organization; not just about how to mitigate risk, but how to really become a resilient organization and thrive above the threat through implementation of sound business practices.

2.3 Human Behavior

Organizational understanding must focus not just on the technological factors, but also on the human factors including behavior. Human behavior is the center to the problem of insider threat. I cannot stress this point enough. Understanding current behavior, modifying that behavior as needed, and predicting future behavior is necessary to mitigate risk to the organization. Human behavior is complex, but not entirely unpredictable, especially for the masses.

The role that big data may play in the future is worth exploring at the organizational level. It is necessary to recognize that human resource management needs to interface and be intimately connected with the chief information officer and the entire organization where strategic level implementation will help bring about change to sustain a high level of proficiency in this high-risk area of insider threat.

Speaking of big data, in the technological age we (at least many of us) provide our data to many sources including on social media. Recent privacy compromises were found by the sharing of data from Facebook to third-party users without permission. This had Facebook CEO Mark Zuckerberg testifying and apologizing before Congress in April 2018. Congressional lawmakers addressed such issues to include user privacy, release of 87 million users' data, Russian propaganda, illegal opioid sales. Zuckerberg, unlike OPM leadership, stated, "It was my mistake, I'm sorry. I started Facebook, I run it, and I'm responsible for what happens here." Also stating that "I think there are a number of areas of content we need to do a better job of policing on our service."[10] Since that testimony, in September 2018 a hacker gained access to 50 million Facebook accounts, including the digital security key that enables access to other users' applications;

Facebook immediately took action to remediate potential user risk, however faces fines in Europe.

In the workplace, it has been my experience that people are generally interested in taking care of themselves first, and then secondary interests will be an aim. When the mission of the organization is a good match, or the compensation is a good match, then it can be a win-win for an organizational entity. Employees often do seek out a satisfactory work environment, however many employees will simply take the job that they can get, or the job that will pay them the salary they need, despite having other interests. In the end, the employee's position may not align well to their core values, and compensation and benefits packages may also be misaligned. Employees that are not happy may be more likely to make errors or engage in deliberate sabotage and become vengeful; this is not to say that employees will do this, but some will. Those who are happy and virtuous will still make errors that may in turn be costly to the organization.

Knowing and assessing organizational work culture is very important to strategies that address the mitigation of risk. Although in my line of work, I normally don't quote field manuals from the U.S. Army, I learned the Army's 11 principles of leadership while helping someone study for an exam many years ago and I think those principles apply. First published in 1948, these principles are still taught today.[11] One of these principles is to *know your people and to look out for their welfare*; another, relevant to human behavior is to *set the example* and to *develop a sense of responsibility among your people*. It may be time to go back to some basics, especially to know your people. Knowing your people, in my interpretation, means to know the people like the virtuous and the wicked employees so that they won't make choices that place the organization and their jobs at a greater risk. Setting a leadership example and developing a sense of responsibility among an organization's people should help to build the trust where employees can report concerns before they escalate to create even more open doors and breaches. This type of leadership behavior is likely to help achieve a higher level of positive influence on the workforce. A turnover rate within an organization can be an indicator of dissatisfaction, however there can be a lot of indicators on the state of an organization's wellness. Behavior is an area that this book will continue to reinforce, to achieve a greater depth of understanding to the problems and the solutions. Again it is a risk decision. Hiring and firing employees can be financially costly, and will likely have many secondary and/or cascading impacts in the workplace.

A traditional human resources staffing model can be depicted in several ways, however the model I'm most familiar with may be depicted with a cyclical process. Different academic authors and practitioners will have slightly different models. Some staffing models have had stricter guidelines because of equal employment opportunity laws which can extend to having broader recruitment campaigns.

The following is an innovative flow process of how I see an optimal state of a relevant staffing cycle. An increase in knowing the employee and understanding behavior patterns overall and knowing how people do tasks is important to reducing risk to insider threat, because good employees, even overly helpful employees, including strategic human resources staff also make mistakes. Threats that organizations face occur in both the public and private sectors in government and industry. These threats exist in common, are often shared, and include both service and information system infrastructure. According to the National Cyber Security Division of U.S. Department of Homeland Security, the infrastructure system has shown the need for innovation in the creation of roles, responsibilities, and competencies for an information technology workforce.

2.3.1 Staffing Cycle to Minimize Insider Threat

Below is an example staffing cycle that might be incorporated, or adapted into an existing cycle to provide additional mitigation of risk against insider threat. Where some of the staffing cycle elements will be familiar, some additional steps should be required for traditional security as well as cybersecurity. Mitigating risk up front will be important to the overall bottom line. The following is such an example.

1. *Establishment of a position*
   - Establishing a functional requirement
   - Develop a position description and require recurring funding that includes adequate technological reinvestment

- Ensure all organizational positions functionally require basic levels of traditional security and cybersecurity knowledge
- Understand the competitive nature or risk landscape of the area of employment or specialization of the position

2. *Recruitment and screening*
   - Organization considers and applies recruitment outreach methods
   - Organization screening of candidates through survey and interview
   - Background checks and verification of prior employment
   - Be wary of reports of narcissism and unchecked reported behavior
   - Include pretests that may include basic cybersecurity screening and best security practices in general
   - Personality inventories may be included in some cases, when particular traits may have been identified as being at higher risk; this may depend on the type of organization

3. *Selection and preemployment training*
   - Final selection
   - Explanation of security protocols during screening
   - Inform of social media protocols, limitations of personal technology use related to work
   - Basic cybersecurity training including various accountability agreements such as non-disclosure agreements
   - Organizational acclimation
   - Position training, as necessary
   - Employee feedback loop established
   - Organizational transparency communications when possible
   - Explanation of standing benefits, and any options or perks that are linked to performance

4. *Employee–employer relationship-building phase*
   - Transparency and organizational communications
   - Team building and fostering a culture of respect
   - Performance management; increased attention during times of poor performance, referral to benefits, and attention to behavior

- Rewards and recognition
- Individual development and training
- Yearly employee feedback loop (such as survey)
- Ongoing evaluation of organizational requirements for position including cybersecurity testing and evaluation

5. *Termination phase*
   - Expect to place heightened security toward the end of employment
   - Policy in place to cover various forms of end of employment (voluntary, involuntary, retirement, death)
   - Credential revocations including computer privileges
   - Potential for immediate access denial
   - Review of any non-disclosure forms
   - Informing, where applicable relevant security offices and other internal stakeholders
   - Employee exit survey. Really pay attention to this. Is the employee leaving happily, and might they be vengeful? If they are leaving in a negative way, is someone else in the organization an unchecked catalyst?

2.4 Tangible Loss

Tangible loss may be perceived, specifically measured, or appraised. In cybersecurity it can be difficult to estimate true losses since impacts can simply be perception, and therefore an opportunity cost or potential customer base is lost. While insurance companies have a good handle on traditional, leaning toward more physical security and risk, cybersecurity is not as easily insured against. Risk can not necessarily be shifted in this area, or the stakes are so high, that insurance policies may not pay out well. Policies that protect against cyber-crimes exist, but can be extremely limited. There is just so much damage that can be done that it is too difficult to measure for those who provide the policies. As an alternative, there are companies that can be purchased on retainer to provide forensics and other crisis management protocols related to cybersecurity.

This trend will likely continue as hackers become increasingly aggressive. For example, in early 2016 a Hollywood, California, hospital was hacked and their information technology systems taken over;

ransom demands were made before hackers would release the digital record system back to the hospital. Beyond the massive potential privacy leak issues, the hospital had to deal with frozen-in technology capabilities where many reported observers speculated that backup systems may have been nonexistent. Although more is to be learned about this particular case in the future, the hospital administrators selected to pay $17,000[12] in bitcoin to get their system back. Ransomware is a form of extortion and an output from the field of cryptovirology.

The Federal Bureau of Investigations continues to investigate this hack, and others; although ransom attacks have not been as common as other tactics and this may have been the first time a hospital hack of this magnitude and tactic has been reported. However, the tactic often works, and succumbing to these types of demands has since established a lucrative precedent for hackers. The U.S. Department of Health and Human Services has taken serious note, breaches also violate protected health information and there have been increasing reports of these types of attacks to a staggering tune of over 4000 daily attacks being launched since 2016.[13] Typically, when ransoms are paid, encryption keys are provided; however, ransomware may also be launched with other malware that destroys.

Emerging victims of this tactic though ransomware are several U.S. police departments; showing the boldness of these hackers who have held hostage police records with encryption; out-of-date systems with vulnerabilities making them easier targets for attack.[14] I recently attended a local police capabilities demonstration and toured a mobile emergency response command post, which was very out-of-date technologically. Where many funds flowed to local law enforcement immediately following 9/11, those grants have been drastically reduced, many technology security investments are not understood by local council members that ultimately vote on budgets with limited resources. Unfortunately, the old mental model of something still working to keep it running is not a secure option with computer technology.

Patient medical records have been breached in other facilities, either through hacking open doors or through other insider threat vulnerabilities. For example, as a case of perhaps virtuous or wicked insider threat, documents have been left in cars or other open areas and subsequently stolen. This was the case in San Antonio, Texas where in 2011 an U.S. Army case manager left medical records of thousands of military soldiers and family in a car during the work-day, and they were taken.[15] Again and again, these stories continue to make headlines indicating that insider threat is a persistent threat that needs ongoing assessment and mitigation of this risk.

Investment is being made by organizations in technology security on technology protections, but they must not forget to invest in thwarting against the human risk element. Research a decade ago focused on the practical consequences of increased connectivity and reliance on information technology as one of being exposed to greater information systems threat and risk.[16] As technology growth has continued, this practical knowledge should also grow, if it is prioritized by organizations.

2.5 Policy Gaps

It does very little for an organization if a policy does not exist, or if a policy does exist and is not known to workers, or is not translated into meaningful and useable language for employees (despite what the policy writers think) or others that operate within the organization. Policies that are able to be interpreted by interdisciplinary employees in the same way are essential; however, this as you might expect can be difficult. If a policy is not clearly understood, this is the equivalent of not having the policy itself, or worse. Starting with an organizational doctrine is an important way forward, as it can help to organize challenges and formulate approaches based on current conditions that the organization operates in.

Doctrine does not have to be lengthy, but it can provide a succinct framework for organizational leaders to guide employees toward a common culture. A risk-informed culture that receives risk communications will be more resilient, especially when managing virtuous, wicked, and vengeful insider threat behaviors. This will also need to be achieved through training and capability development, which includes ensuring security standards are met for all employees (and expanded definition of employees') area of responsibility. Policy should be considered holistically to include historical context and existing strategy. Sometimes saying "do as I say" will work, but often employees might want to know why, or seriously question when leaders do just the opposite. Employees might ask why a policy needs to be a particular way, because from a systems perspective not everyone can see the entire system and the reason it must function the way it does or should. Policy should be rooted to some meaningful doctrine purpose, it should have a nexus to a law or regulation; or tied in with or be about the vision of the chief executive officer; or about accountability to the stakeholders or the purpose of the company; all should be directly linked in with the organization's values and be strategically communicated. Remember that if you have properly hired through your improved staffing cycle, following policy should come more easily; however, monitoring should never be eliminated.

Without having doctrine actually codified in written form, there is a possibility that unwritten misinformed doctrine can guide an organization, even if the unofficial doctrine does not fully represent the organizational intent. Doctrine can be thought of as a central belief system that informs strategy; it is a dynamic relationship. Organizational doctrine can codify best practices, convey belief systems, and serve as a foundation for risk management and informed communications (Table 2.2). Ideally, doctrine should articulate the best way forward considering historical context, best practices, exercises, and critical analysis. Doctrine should somehow incorporate culture, even if it means to change it. Continuous strategic messaging is important, especially when organizational change is underway. Telecommunications policy, including cybersecurity/information assurance that might have been in place for several years, may not be good enough today, nor be adequate enough to move you and your organization forward into the future. Ensuring that you have the right technology strategists in place, as well as policy experts, is increasingly important.

Table 2.2 Doctrine and Risk Management

DOCTRINE CAN:
• Unify an organization under a common risk management umbrella and cohesive understanding.
• Create organizational best practices for institutionalizing risk management culture (including best practices and lessons learned).
• Establish a formalized, recurring process for evaluating and mitigating risks through a deliberate process to identify and assess assets in order to further establish processes to mitigate risks.
• Create a common understanding of how risk management informs decision making.

Note, however, that technology advances that affect capabilities can also create a misalignment of strategy and doctrine, so a fresh look and ongoing flow of lessons learned, best practices, and reassessment should occur on a formalized basis so that doctrine may continue to be relevant and informative for future organizational strategy. Policy should strongly rely on looking at after-action reports and lessons learned in order to identify potential changes that should occur.

As discussed, many changes occurred after Hurricane Katrina. Here is one change you may be less familiar with. There were many pet owners who would not leave their pets behind for evacuation purposes, and as a result many people stayed behind, and sadly in some cases perished. If an evacuee chose to leave and left their pets behind, many of these pets suffered and died from the harsh conditions or starved to death in locked homes. Because of the lessons learned from Hurricane Katrina, the importance of pets was elevated, and Congress passed the Pets and Evacuation Transportation Standards Act of 2006.[17] Both animal welfare and the belief system that pets were important to people allowed systemic changes, and required states that requested FEMA to also support at a higher level the safety of pets.

Leaning forward and finding flexibility in solutions will be important into the future. Technology requires an adaptability that not all aspects of an organization will be used to, nor will particular acquisitions processes likely be aligned. Realizing this challenge now will help you to organize for success now and well into the future. Gaps in policy areas were specifically described to include nonexistent information technology security policy. Policies are not intended to be shelfware but are action documents; employees need to be notified of them, know where to retrieve them, and know when they have been adjusted or changed. Creating an easily accessible document library or having a standardized policy area will be important that documents be shared organizationally to minimize policy gaps.

An organizational policy addressing the prevention insider threat would not necessarily be inherently known to the employee without effective communications about what insider threat is, unless this was a topic that was covered initially as part of prescreening. I assert that most employees do not necessarily recognize their behaviors as risky; however, ignorance will continue to perpetuate very preventable insider threat situations, especially for the virtuous and the wicked insider.

2.6 Finance and Logistic Challenges

Along with knowing that your assets need security, knowing what your assets are is equally important, especially in larger organizations which can be more difficult to get a handle on. No matter the size of an organization, there is a high probability that both financial and logistical challenges will need to be tackled as related to insider threat. If your IT investment has not been centrally managed, what you may come to discover is that you likely have a number of kingdoms, not necessarily by design, but by growth over time that might have remained unchecked or simply have become obsolete but continue to function. Some IT systems may even be off the radar completely. It is critically important to obtain a comprehensive understanding of your IT capability, not just the count of your assets as with property, but from a security standpoint as well, in order to secure the needed protection.

Information technology security relics may be limited in capability. By knowing how IT is managed and/or centralized, you may discover extra funding and resources to bring your network under a standardized configuration; exceptions should undergo a review process that are subsequently tracked and centrally managed. It is recognized that when exceptions do occur, specialized support will need to go along with these resources in some cases so that new risks are not introduced into the network.

Information technology specialists can be very good in supporting IT system operations, but may change configurations, that place systems at risk, to support a software purchase that might be desirable but not necessary to business functionality. Without an investment board or a control board with oversight of non-standard adjustments, an organization will soon be fraught with unknown threat and unmitigated risk. Standard configuration and centralized funding and investment management is key, assuming that particular security protocols that are being implemented are correct. Indeed, there needs to be a way to trust but verify. If a security team is not technically capable of these verify assessments, this introduces an entire new set of problems. Simply saying yes and not being able to competently verify puts an organization at risk. It is an illusion of compliance, an illusion of monitoring, testing, and evaluating compliance.

Recapitalization of computers has become increasingly important. The management of computers needs to shift, if it has not already, to that not of an asset management system like a property item, but that of an asset that must be updated, managed, patched, and be mission ready. Computer recapitalization is very important and is a shift from an IT maintenance mindset of fix it until it can't be fixed anymore. This is a paradigm shift with a financial implication in that it costs a lot of money to continually recapitalize. That balance point of risk versus obsolescence and increased compromise or unsupported technology needs to be properly balanced.

I was recently at a luncheon where a woman in the private sector serving in a marketing position treated her work computer as if it were an open public computer. Essentially, she treated it as if she were at a public terminal, because she had no assurance that the security features were current and that there hadn't been a key logger that had been placed on her terminal to capture all of her computer strokes. This made me think "wow, there are a lot of businesses that still do not protect their terminals and their employees feel they are at risk." Can you imagine if a client's information is stored on such a terminal, and what type of risk that might place a client? I just shook my head a bit, but I'm sure this is not an isolated story, especially with small business.

2.7 Information Mismanagement

Not having accurate data or an understanding what data to collect or look at can be problematic. If you have a scorecard, but that scorecard measures a sliver of what the true cybersecurity wellness picture really is, then that is only an illusion of security, and your organization will remain at high-risk. Protecting data is important from a competitive advantage, and also from a corporate responsibly perspective or requirement that can vary depending on the nature and location of an organization's business. From a strategic standpoint, a Government Accountability Office (GAO) audit in 2015 looked at small agencies with less than 6,000 employees and assessed them against criteria established for cybersecurity and privacy.[18] While the GAO audit findings were relatively mediocre with mixed results, the categorical assessment is an excellent starting point for any organization.

Table 2.3   Strengthening Information Security and Privacy Programs

IMPLEMENTATION ASSESSMENT (STRATEGIC LEVEL)	ORGANIZATIONAL IMPLEMENTATION RATING FULL, PARTIAL, OR NOT AT ALL
INFORMATION SECURITY	
Risk assessments	Full, partial, no implementation
Policies and procedures	Full, partial, no implementation
Security training program	Full, partial, no implementation
Continuous monitoring of security controls	Full, partial, no implementation
Remediation program	Full, partial, no implementation
Incident response and reporting	Full, partial, no implementation
Continuity of operations program	Full, partial, no implementation
[*Acquisitions and IT security, pre/during/post contract] *author added.	Full, partial, no implementation
PRIVACY ELEMENTS	
Issue system of records notices	Full, partial, no implementation
Assign senior agency official for privacy	Full, partial, no implementation
Conduct privacy impact assessments	Full, partial, no implementation

Assessment worksheet: practical application: circle current state.

Basic cybersecurity hygiene is extremely important. The measures reflected requirements as required by the Federal Information Security Management Act of 2002, the Privacy Act of 1974, and the E-Government Act of 2002, among other guidance by the Office of Management and Budget. The following is drawn so that you may review your organization at a strategic level, against the criteria presented (Table 2.3).

One of the items not summarized that I would absolutely add is attention within the acquisitions process, not just the acquisition, but particular attention to the "process."

2.8 Policing

The concept of policing is clearly linked to that of accountability. It is the organization's responsibility to ensure that individuals understand what their authorities are in formally accepting accountability on behalf of their organization. Position power alone may not give a person the required authority to accept the risks, change configurations, and audit controls. Policing might be more easily understood with applying some physical protection standards. Within professional physical protection standards there are clear entry and exit checkpoints along with credential validation; however, with technology, these entrance and exit points may or may not be actually guarded.

The reality is that there are a lot of entry and exit points within a system, especially those systems that have a nexus directly with the internet. Even organizations that did not believe they had a nexus were surprised to find that employees, through Wi-Fi connectivity, had created doorways they were not aware of. I attended a transportation security forum where the example of a prison system hacking was discussed. As the scenario goes, the lead researcher with a small team easily purchased software—though it could have been acquired without the legitimate purchase—and was able to exploit the computer system vulnerabilities further, discovering how to open all the prison doors. Prisons often use programmable logic controllers, devices are similar to the ones that were exploited with Stuxnet.[19] After the prison system leadership was informed of this high-level security breach, details of this specific project was later published in *Wired* magazine. This vulnerability was created by a likely virtuous insider who had created an access point through a wireless connection. These particular devices have been around for some time; however, the focus has been on larger Supervisory Control and Data Acquisition Systems (SCADA).

SCADA is used for remote monitoring and control of systems; these larger systems can generally be found in various infrastructure sectors throughout the United States and the globe at large, such as in the energy and water sectors. A SCADA is a type of industrial control system that remotely monitors and controls processes that exist in the physical world; these sites are often operated in multiple locations and over distance. Indeed, SCADA may have radio, satellite, and wired connections and many of these can have built in encryption. Intruders will obtain access to these control signals and sabotage them to critical points of failure.

Policing is also about ensuring that response reactions and implementing restrictions do not cause more harm than good. This might be a temporary decision-making judgment before a longer-term solution or an investment is found in another form of security control. Some of these controls can be expensive, but the trade-off is over the longer term.

Although standards need to be in place, particular circumstances should be reviewed before a system is simply shut down. One user should not have the ability to take down an entire organization, and if it does, well there is another risk for human resource management to resolve. The risk of shutting a system down when an active attack is underway could potentially be greater than isolating a risk at a node, like creating a dam that diverts one stream, and creates a barrier to allow a main system to continue working. In smaller organizations, there may be a possibility that there are fewer redundancies put into the system, so a major disruption could have a cascading impact on other systems. This links directly with knowing what assets you have, where they are connected to the larger system, and where connections may not be entirely visible.

The human forensic understanding, being able to view and understand and to make the physical and cyber connections, continues to be important, and this need for a cyber-savvy workforce is only going to continue. The need for accountability and policing in the cyber-security domain will also continue to grow. All insiders are a threat, and all must be held accountable from the most junior employee to the most senior executive employee in an organization. Organizations should establish a warning system up to a zero tolerance for particular incidents that occur. Consequences should not simply be politics as usual. These are small errors that can lead to and have huge organizational consequences.

For example, in 2018, a computer-user error had the Hawaii Emergency Management Agency and the State of Hawaii scrambling because of an actual warning that was released instead of a test alert regarding incoming missiles.[20] There was no way to recall the message, and the time lapse between the actual warning and the redacting of this erroneous warning was delayed more than half an hour because there was no process set up to recall the warning. Although the computer technician was reassigned, the reality is that the system the technician was working in was flawed, with limited process controls. Although this was a virtuous error, it was larger representation of outdated technology and a lot of panic.

2.9 Time as a Threat Consideration

The concept of time has not been well documented in consequence definitions. The definition of consequence has been illustrated for the most part, to think in terms of causes and reactions, which are generally more immediate. Let's say there is a weather event, such as a hurricane, you will have a shorter term response followed by a longer term resilience recovery to the area. Although a longer-term economic impact might be felt, this is often looked at as part of known expectations. Consequences are often thought of as being direct; it is the direct aftermath impact of the storm and the resilience in bouncing back, for example. However, in cybersecurity, consequences can be delayed, and the awareness of the cyber event, or cyber-related compromise or circumstances, not easily determined, nor immediately known. The result can occur well into the future and well after the hack or compromise has occurred. In the U.S. culture, we are generally very good responders (with some exception), however systems often don't get fixed before it is viewed as broken; again, the paradigm shift that was previously discussed. With cybersecurity, ensuring something is within security control standards is increasingly important. Systems have to be reinforced, and strengthened then removed from the networks even before they are broken to keep up with the increased threats. Redistribution of resources is likely necessary to ensure this high standard is kept. Cyber-related attacks can be immediate, but they can also be delayed, during which time collection of information can occur, or strategy can be developed on how to best exploit the organization that has been intruded upon. It is possible that there will be a time delay on attack, where an adversary will select a time of greater weakness for exploitation, including being able to gain access to prepare for a future attack. That access could also be obtained through physical connections. Both traditional security and cybersecurity are intricately linked, and it is of the utmost importance that they be considered linked together and not at polar opposites, as previously discussed.

2.10 Theoretical Discussion Turned into Practical Mental Models

Mental models are beneficial for conceptualization of complex topics. By now, you should see that the creation of a new definition of insider threat has started to evolve and be applied. Throughout this book I will present 10 mental models that are all aspects of a *Grounded Theory of Insider Cyber Threat*. The chapters will continue to build your understanding of this definition and conceptualization with very practical application. The creation of a new understanding of insider cybersecurity threat to organization is being revealed for you.

2.10.1 Mental Model (Aspect 1)—At the Crossroads

An initial mental model that I refer to as *Aspect 1 as a grounded theory aspect of insider threat, the phenomenon of crossroads convergence at the medium.* As an explanation of this theory development, I micro-analyzed the concept of *social engineering,* and this led to further examining the act of *trickery* by a perpetrator, which in turn led to an understanding that both good and bad employees can be tricked, and the commonality of risk was at the organizational entry point. This idea was a concept that expanded the construct of internal and external to a middle ground, or *medium,* essentially the crossroads on the edge-of-in, and the edge-of-out (of an organization). Ultimately this micro-analysis was the catalyst for the construction of the grounded theory of insider threat, the phenomenon of crossroads convergence at the medium, which I refer to as *Mental Model (Aspect 1)—At the Crossroads.*

2.10.2 Mental Model (Aspect 2)—The Virtuous and the Wicked

The next mental model I call *Aspect 2,* which is a *grounded theory aspect of the phenomenon of the virtuous employee and the wicked employee, as a risk of insider threat to organization.* This is a new way of thinking about insider threat to organization. The distinction between a virtuous employee and a wicked employee in the context of insider cybersecurity threat was not found in the literature until now. There are several layers to this concept. The medium described as *Aspect 1* is a middle ground where all employees potentially, despite their intentions—the good, the bad, and the ugly—can be tricked. An insider threat of trickery discovered at the crossroads where the good employee and the bad employee are both susceptible to meet with this trickery demon. This place is at the edge of the organization and at the edge of outside the organization, a new medium where threats may enter and employees may let them.

Separate from the sameness of the virtuous and the wicked employee being tricked, there are distinctions between the two. The virtuous employee is an employee trying to do the right thing in conducting their day-to-day activities, but blissfully unaware of their risky behaviors; the virtuous employee will work outside of the best practices known to security professionals, but these risks remain unknown to the employee, who proceeds to work each day wearing innocent lenses. This is a contrast with the wicked employee who knows they are making a deliberate deviation from best practices. Organizational culture may shape a virtuous employee's perspective to believe that what they are doing is acceptable and good, when it really is not from an organizational security perspective, and is instead risky human behavior especially if policy and security managers are not in position. Several of these behaviors are presented in the next chapter as the typologies of human behavior risk factors that influence or contribute to the outcome of unintended insider threat.

The wicked employee is considered an employee that is creating a work-around, and the employee knows that this work-around may not be consistent with policy, or the conditions of their employment. Organizational culture may also shape a wicked employee's perspective to believe that some of what they are doing is acceptable, because of the greater good (such as loading unauthorized software that will benefit one organizational unit). However, it is really not from an organizational security perspective, and is instead risky human behavior. There are ranges of wicked. For example, on the one hand, wicked employees are not deliberately trying to maliciously harm the organization even though they are not following the rules. Wicked employees may even understand that there could be some loss or damage. This loss may be viewed as acceptable to the wicked employee, and at times his or her supervisors. A wicked employee, on the other hand, may also circumvent the system to benefit their own interests, which are significantly counter to the organizational mission. In more extreme cases, this could include setting up fictitious accounts, creating remote access to other computers or networks to play video games, or watch pornography, for example. Secondary or tertiary consequences could still emerge from the behavior of the wicked employee that may not have been considered beforehand, or simply ignored by the wicked employee. In some cases, a wicked employee could be a privileged user with higher-access control levels.

2.10.3 In Review

The insider threat definition of who may be an insider was developed to include all insiders, any human employee (temporary, volunteer), surrogate employee, or third party (such as contractor, service provider, vendor, or inside user of a product or service) that could have virtual or physical access. This finding is an indicator that organizations should take the time to frequently renew their organizational access and connections to more fully understand and define who their insiders really are. This may extend beyond original constructs, depending on the organization (Figure 2.1).

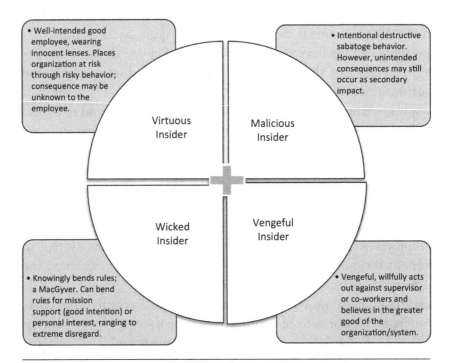

• Well-intended good employee, wearing innocent lenses. Places organization at risk through risky behavior; consequence may be unknown to the employee.

• Intentional destructive sabotoge behavior. However, unintended consequences may still occur as secondary impact.

Virtuous Insider

Malicious Insider

Wicked Insider

Vengeful Insider

• Knowingly bends rules; a MacGyver. Can bend rules for mission support (good intention) or personal interest, ranging to extreme disregard.

• Vengeful, willfully acts out against supervisor or co-workers and believes in the greater good of the organization/system.

Figure 2.1   All insiders are a threat to organization.

Explained further is additional reflectivity on a very basic common set of investigatory prompts: *who, what, when, where, why*, and *how*, in order to grasp an even better understanding of the complex topic, and how to present the insider threat; assessment and mitigation of risks with more insightful flow for the reader.

Who. The *who* is the insider, a human entity, and perhaps an artificial intelligence, although this is at a more prototype level, though with time could become a greater threat. The human is also the gatekeeper, whether they realize it or not; the gatekeeper for the organization. As a gatekeeper, the insider may actually open doors to invite outsiders in; intentionally or unintentionally without understanding or partly understanding, the consequences. For conceptualization purposes, this is a door, not as one that can simply be opened and closed; instead it is a revolving door. The access point more of a space suspended between open and closed, that point where you have left the other room, but have not yet entered the next. Although this may be viewed as a threshold, I have deliberately made a different language choice that infers a greater description that applies to the physical and the virtual. Of course, one room could easily be 2,000 miles away, but yet the door connects the two, a portal gateway if you will. I call this middle point or area the medium. A grounded theory of insider threat, the phenomenon of crossroads convergence at the medium.

What. The *what* is the insider threat itself, either intended or unintended. This threat is the result of some action, or failure to act that has an intended or unintended consequence. The action that may be a catalyst action is likely to be an engagement of risky behavior that leads to a tangible loss, whether or not that loss is understood or even discovered due to potentially unseen cascading impacts. A distinction that was raised during the study is that some threat could be unintended, even if the initial action stemmed from a separate intended action meant to be vengeful, or even malicious, but with a different target. Doors (physical or virtual) could also be opened that allow other threats to occur, despite the fact they were not originally intending to open those particular doors for that particular threat. So indeed, unintended insider threat could even stem from a malicious act with a completely different intent; though the focus of this study does not fully explore this aspect, and it would be expected to be covered as a by-product of vengeful or malicious intent.

When. The *when* is the timing of the threat compromise, which can occur at any time, the threat may have a lag time to become manifest. This means anytime, 24/7. Consequences are normally considered to be more immediate in resultant impacts, connected to known events; however, this is not necessarily the case, especially when dealing with information technology security. Large amounts of data and important knowledge can be retrieved and stored for future use, or can go unnoticed for years. Manifestations of threats do not simply wait for the Monday to Friday, 7:00 a.m. to 4:00 p.m. time to attack, however, employees working during this time could certainly leave doors open during this time, to be later exploited.

Where. The *where* is the location from which the insider threat originates, and this can exist anywhere. The threat may exist in a physical location, a virtual location, an operational mission engagement abroad, at home working, at work working, on the road working, or at play in social activities in both the virtual or physical worlds. The origination can be anywhere in the world, the geographical boundaries extended into the virtual. The threat can manifest when it has access to the organization. In order to better understand the where, better understanding the various parts of an organization is also important. Events could be a catalyst for this. For example, employees that might normally be careful may lower their guard when they are being furloughed, or being forced to move out of their positions because of significant organizational changes. A furlough is a forced layoff, often unpaid, and may be manifested from budget cuts; this has been seen in recent years for a number of federal agencies in the United States. Employees may feel slighted or vengeful when they are turned away at the door after having worked for decades for an organization and then simply not permitted to go to their desks. This could have a psychological impact on the individual. Reorganization can also unintentionally leave individuals with bruised egos and dashed dreams.

Why. The *why* is the reason why insider threat occurs. It covers both intended and unintended insider threat. Unintended insider threat is an area, as described earlier, that has been less known up to this point. There are several human factors relating to insider threat to information technology systems and the organization at large. The threat may also become realized due to inadequate organizational support mechanisms, including inadequacy of policing such as information assurance and other internal and external internal audit control mechanisms.

How. The *how* may be described as the action of people engaging in manifest or latent risky behavior, or in the prioritization of organizational resources or vision. The virtuous and the wicked employee, is distinctly different from vengeful and malicious in the conscious level of engaging—the how. Increased attention to internal controls, logistics and finance process and decisions, as well as policy and doctrine, strategic information management and collaboration, and leadership approaches will also impact the how. The level of enterprise wide monitoring and policing activity will influence how organizations will be able to identify how insider threat occurs, and to mitigate risks from all insider types, and respond to actual events when they occur.

Appendix: Best Practice—Practical Knowledge and Practitioner Application

Practical knowledge

- Ensure you recognize the ideological shift to the four categories of insiders. The virtuous, wicked, vengeful, and malicious.
- Ensure you recognize that all insiders are a threat. Understand who your insiders are, what and how they access.
- Understand how the insider threat programs should be more comprehensive.

- Understand the importance of organizational strategy, doctrine, and policy related to cybersecurity at large, and insider threat in particular including physical security.
- Recognize the usefulness of mental models to strategically communicate risk.

Practitioner application

- Ensure you know your dynamic insider threat risk landscape and are able to build in flexibility to respond to the changing environment.
- Review the Core Category checklist, assign organizational leads, co-leads, and determine controls and accountability. Assess and identify any organizational gaps.
- Establish a regular process to review and update doctrine, strategy, and policy based on lessons learned. Establish a cyber strategy that addresses both internal and external influences, including an interdisciplinary insider threat program.
- Use cybersecurity and privacy implementation assessment worksheet.
- Start cultivating a risk-informed culture while placing controls and accountability that will mitigate risk.
- Focus on building a resilient workforce through strategic communications.

Endnotes

1. Bradley Manning Sentenced to 35 Years in WikiLeaks Case, by J. Tate, *Washington Post.* August 21, 2013. Retrieved from www.washington-post.com.
2. I Knew Chelsea Manning in Basic Combat Training. Here's the Story You Haven't Heard by Jay B. Huwieler. Retrieved from https://huwieler.net/2017/01/18/chelsea-manning-in-basic-combat-training/.
3. U.S. Department of State, Bureau of Security and Nonproliferation. Retrieved from https://www.state.gov/t/isn/index.htm.
4. Santos, E., Nguyen, H., Yu, F., Kim, K.J., Li, D., Wilkinson, J.T., Olson, A., Russell, J., & Clark, B. (2011). Intelligence analysis and the insider threat. *IEEE Transactions on Systems, Man and Cybernetics, Part A: Systems and Humans*, 42, 331–347. doi:10.1109/TSMCA.2011.2162500.

5. The White House, Office of the Press Secretary Background Conference Call on the Policy Changes in Cuba and on the Release of Alan Gross. December 17, 2014. Retrieved from https://www.whitehouse. gov/the-press-office/2014/12/17/background-conference-call-policy-changes-cuba-and-release-alan-gross.

6. The White House, Office of the Press Secretary Fact Sheet: Charting a New Course on Cuba. December 17, 2014. Retrieved from https://www.whitehouse.gov/the-press-office/2014/12/17/fact-sheet-charting-new-course-cuba.

7. Memorandum from the Office of the Inspector General, to Acting Director U.S. Office of Personnel Management. July 22, 2015. Retrieved from www.U.S. Office of Personnel Management.gov.

8. Castro: U.S. Hasn't Responded to Katrina Offer by Newman, L. CNN. September 5, 2005. Retrieved from http://www.cnn.com/2005/WORLD/americas/09/05/katrina.cuba/.

9. U.S. Department of Homeland Security. Disasters Overview. 2015. Retrieved from https://www.dhs.gov/disasters-overview.

10. Zuckerburg Apologizes to Congress for Data Scrape—Which Also Grabbed His Facebook Information by Tony Romm. April 11, 2018. *Washington Post*. Retrieved from https://www.washingtonpost.com/news/the-switch/wp/2018/04/11/zuckerberg-facebook-hearing-congress-house-testimony/?utm_term=.58a3d2a50de0.

11. 11 Timeless Principles of Leadership (U.S. Army, 1948) by Deierlien, T. 2014. Retrieved from http://www.academyleadership.com/news/201406.asp.

12. Hollywood Hospital Pays $1700 in Bitcoin to Hackers: FBI investigating by Winton, R. *Los Angeles Times.* February 18, 2016. Retrieved from http://touch.latimes.com/#section/-1/article/p2p-85937755/.

13. U.S. Department of Health and Human Services. Ransomware and HIPAA. 2018. Retrieved from https://www.hhs.gov/hipaa/for-professionals/security/guidance/cybersecurity/index.html.

14. Ransomware Hackers Blackmail U.S. Police Departments by Francescani, Chris. April 26, 2016. Retrieved from https://www.nbcnews.com/news/us-news/ransomware-hackers-blackmail-u-s-police-departments-n561746.

15. Office of Inadequate Security; Your Info, Their Screw-Ups. Retrieved from www.databreaches.net.

16. Walters, L. M. (2007). A draft of an information systems security and control course. *Journal of Information Systems*, 21(1), 123–148. doi:10-2308/jis.2007.21.1.123.

17. How Hurricane Katrina Turned Pets into People by David Grimm. July 31, 2015. Retrieved from https://www.buzzfeed.com/davidhgrimm/how-hurricane-katrina-turned-pets-into-people?utm_term=.noE4XEY96m#.giop6Y3K8Z.

18. Government Accountability Report on Information Security. U.S. Government Accountability Office, Report GAO-14-344. June 2014. Retrieved from www.gao.gov.

19. Researchers say vulnerabilities could let hackers spring prisoners from cells by Zetter, K. *Wired*. July 29, 2011. Retrieved from http://www.wired.com/2011/07/prison-plc-vulnerabilities/.

20. Hawaii Missile Alert: How One Employee "Pushed the Wrong Button" and Caused a Wave of Panic by Amy Wang. January 14, 2018. *Washington Post*. Retrieved from https://www.washingtonpost.com/news/post-nation/wp/2018/01/14/hawaii-missile-alert-how-one-employee-pushed-the-wrong-button-and-caused-a-wave-of-panic/?utm_term=.b2a20cb50719.

3

ORGANIZATIONAL RISK FACTORS FOR UNINTENDED INSIDER THREAT

3.1 Introduction

An ideological shift must be made in terms of insider threat so that more aggressive and more thoughtful mitigation techniques can be applied in a more holistic manner. This particular chapter addresses risk factors that are not commonly understood, nor likely/frequently considered as part of the insider threat program. The risk factors that contribute directly to unintended insider threat is where a great deal of progress can be made to assess and mitigate risk within organizations. If leadership considers and implements these categories as part of a risk mitigation program, then a better change process along with a greater understanding of their associated mental models, will occur.

A greater depth of understanding is needed for organizations to more comprehensively understand the risk factors that reside within their organizations. How the business work function is conducted today looks significantly differently than it did a generation ago, including outsourcing of work. The option for a significant number of employees or contractors to extend their work environment into the vast world, seemingly anywhere, is now common practice, well beyond the traditional brick-and-mortar walls owned by an organization. Contracts and subcontracts create opportunities in which tasks performed may be far beyond the observation of traditional security protocols where opportunities for response may or may not be immediate. When operating system updates or patch updates are delayed, vulnerabilities may exist when computers are not properly managed or tracked as an asset. Unsupported and out-of-date software, where there are no vulnerability patches, can create havoc very quickly in organizations. Additionally, some work spaces alone may be in higher threat locations such as: at home, on a metro, in a coffee shop, at a remote telework site; hotel bars and lobbies, and other contractor designated work spaces. Globalization has created vast amounts of business that is being conducted on-the-go. The places from where network connections can be established, given the right equipment and passcodes, are seemingly endless. Human behaviors are difficult to monitor by security personnel in such disparate locations, if at all. It is unlikely that this type of remote work will decrease due to increasing population centers. Employers have sought to decrease both their transportation and corporate office carbon footprints by requiring their employees to telework and in some cases offer telework as a benefit in an attempt to retain quality employees.

First, I provide a narrative response, as I did in the preceding chapter, that directly answers what factors contribute to unintended insider threat, then I provide a listing of categories that are displayed in Table 3.1. These categories are listed for readability in terms of core categories as well as their cascading sub-categories. Last, toward the end of the chapter, I enter into a more comprehensive discussion. Throughout the discussion, practical application, mental models and best practices are called out. Specifically, the categories may be used by an organization to identify controls that they should use to mitigate the risk element.

What are the factors that contribute to unintended insider threat? The answers follow.

3.1.1 The Narrative Response

- Unintended insider threat increases with human risky behavior; this behavior is captured into typologies that include the following employee behaviors: transporter carrier; litterer; too-tolerant being; risk revealer; scattered data collector; seldom unexpected; gluttonous optimizer; unknowing curator; defiant disregarder; technically obsolescent; hygiene-hindered communicator; goofing around player; blissful user; trust believer; rushed surge responder; memorable password scribe; privileged user abuser; unmonitored teleworkers; wide-open wanderer; verbal space cadet; unguarded doorman; absentminded; face-off subordinate; shortcut alleyway taker; uninstructed newbie;

surprisingly superhuman; ivory towered; road traveler; part-present, part-timer; storyteller, too-busy-to-tell; not-checked-out employee; the laissez-faire trainee.

- Physical environmental risk factors, coupled with aggravated risk mitigation approaches, and gaps in architectural wellness can lead to increased unintended insider threat risk. Ensuring well-coordinated efforts between physical and cybersecurity mechanisms, including incident response is important. Minimizing the unknown factors among various units/staffs should be a goal. Recognizing that systems may be designed or propagated with error and coordinating to ensure that future changes minimize exposure should also be a goal to minimize unintended insider threat.

3.1.2 The Categorical Response

Now that the narrative has been presented, I will now list the categorical results. These categorical results may be used in terms of an assessment, to identify the organizational responsibility or lead, and assigned control. Following the table is a more descriptive discussion of each of the Core Categories.

Table 3.1 Factors That Contribute to Unintended Insider Threat

CATEGORY	CORE CATEGORY = C, OR SUB-CATEGORY = S	LEAD/CONTROL
Core	A. Human Behavioral Risk Factors Influence or Contribute to the Outcome of Unintended Insider Threat	Suggested type of insider threat with identified typology
S	*Typology 1, the transporter – carrier.* Those who carry data back and forth are more at risk for losing it (transporters, more easily lost, or unattended).	Virtuous, Wicked
S	*Typology 2, the litterer.* People who throw out data or leave things unattended.	Virtuous, Wicked, Vengeful, Malicious
S	*Typology 3, the too-tolerant being.* Humans, such as managers and co-workers allowing others do things they shouldn't.	Virtuous, Wicked, Vengeful
S	*Typology 4, the risk revealer.* Being tricked, social engineered, shoulder surfed. Examples include: intentional disclosure, or unintentional, accidental, office function disclosure such as operational information inappropriately released, writing information that can be compiled into a pattern for gain or other exploitation. Others may be waiting for this person to make a mistake.	Virtuous, Wicked, Vengeful, (Malicious)

(Continued)

Table 3.1 (*Continued*)   Factors That Contribute to Unintended Insider Threat

CATEGORY	CORE CATEGORY = C, OR SUB-CATEGORY = S	LEAD/CONTROL
S	*Typology 5, the scattered data collector.* Collecting information without protection, supply chain consideration, end user, potentially breaking the chain of custody, disruption.	Virtuous, Wicked, (Vengeful)
S	*Typology 6, the seldom unexpected.* Those who do not alter their behavior and are predictable, allowing for others to be familiar.	Virtuous
S	*Typology 7, the gluttonous optimizer.* Seeking gain beyond what is authorized or normal behavior in the work environment may also be convenience motivated.	Wicked
S	*Typology 8, the unknowing curator.* The holder of treasure, or very important things, but unaware of its importance or consequence if compromised. This is an example of someone not aware of immediate or further cascading impacts, should treasure be compromised.	Virtuous
S	*Typology 9, the defiant disregarder.* Ignoring known security practices, or training.	Wicked, Vengeful
S	*Typology 10, the technically obsolescent.* Various levels of this, individuals' technical lack of knowledge or skill to protect data, or unknown reasons.	Virtuous, Wicked
S	*Typology 11, the hygiene-hindered communicator.* Poor receiving and sending hygiene; for example, sending to an unconfirmed agency, person, office, individual, before verifying legitimacy of receiver. May send unprotected when password protection is needed.	Virtuous, Wicked
S	*Typology 12, the goofing around player.* Someone who just plays around to see what they can do, or someone who plays jokes.	Virtuous, Wicked
S	*Typology 13, the blissful user.* Basic and privileged users that have a lack of experience or training.	Virtuous
S	*Typology 14, the trust believer.* Those who are more prone to being socially engineered, or unguarded. Keeping in mind that most everyone can be tricked or a social engineering target. A social engineering targeted attack, also known as spear phishing.	Virtuous
S	*Typology 15, the rushed surge responder.* Missing information assurance factor. Information assurance may decrease during times of immediate incident response, leaving gaps between traditional/physical security and cybersecurity. The needs to provide information may prevail beyond ensuring best security practice will be hierarchical, or externally politically driven.	Wicked

(*Continued*)

Table 3.1 (*Continued*)   Factors That Contribute to Unintended Insider Threat

CATEGORY	CORE CATEGORY = C, OR SUB-CATEGORY = S	LEAD/CONTROL
S	*Typology 16, the memorable password scribe.* The user who cannot remember numerous passwords between home and work, and writes them down, and may transfer back and forth, either online or in person. Collects work and home passwords together.	Virtuous, Wicked
S	*Typology 17, the privileged user abuser.* The ultimate MacGyver work-around with permissions. May create work-around for own benefit to include pornography, gaming, or other interests.	Wicked
S	*Typology 18, the unmonitored teleworker.* This goes beyond work productivity oversight to information security hygiene at home.	Virtuous, Wicked, Vengeful, Malicious (not monitored, could be any)
S	*Typology 19, the wide-open wanderer.* Leaves terminal open or provides access unintentionally or willingly.	Virtuous, Wicked
S	*Typology 20, the verbal space cadet.* In-their-own-world talkers. Those who are on the phone and they ignore physical surroundings and/or are less aware of surroundings and speak too loudly about information that should be protected. This is becoming more common place. Changes in physical space could amplify this—office vs. cubical. Could be seen as loud mouth or overzealous.	Virtuous, Wicked
S	*Typology 21, the unguarded doorman.* More easily allows intrusions, does not question legitimacy of those present physically, nor recognize virtual open doors.	Wicked
S	*Typology 22, the absentminded.* Those who forget small details, not gross negligence.	Virtuous
S	*Typology 23, the face-off subordinate.* Those who dislike their supervisors and do not wilfully make things easy for their supervisor, nor look out for their best interest; outright sabotage, or withholding of vital information for example. The subordinate may still be true to their perception of ethics, and love for the organization.	Vengeful
S	*Typology 24, the shortcut alleyway takers.* Those who want things to be on Easy Street and ignore training and policy.	Wicked
S	*Typology 25, the uninstructed newbie.* Those who are unfamiliar with a particular system. They may not be technologically obsolete but have not had enough experience on a particular system and are not familiar with all of the processes, functions and capabilities of the system including risk in their actions.	Virtuous

(Continued)

Table 3.1 (*Continued*) Factors That Contribute to Unintended Insider Threat

CATEGORY	CORE CATEGORY = C, OR SUB-CATEGORY = S	LEAD/CONTROL
S	*Typology 26, the surprisingly superhuman.* The individual who can hear or see information that they are not supposed to without seeking out this information because of others' behaviors such as talking too loudly.	Virtuous, Wicked, Vengeful, Malicious
S	*Typology 27, the ivory towered.* The user that confuses position status, or other social or ranked privileges, with good information technology hygiene, and may ignore policy. Senior positioned folks (managers, executives, for example) not setting the example, and not adhering to policy.	Wicked
S	*Typology 28, the road traveler.* Using very unsecure networks to access systems, including hotel networks without understanding the associated risks, and not taking precautions to turn off higher risk applications.	Virtuous, Wicked
S	*Typology 29, the part-present part-timer.* Those who are not always present, and don't consider their job primary. Short cuts more frequently taken to access or share data. Data may be repeated on servers throughout the world.	Wicked
S	*Typology 30, the storyteller, too-busy-to-tell.* Storytelling plays a key role in learning organizations. Cybersecurity needs more organizational and timely stories to translate into an analog world in order for more organizational resilience. Lessons learned may be considered part of a story telling.	Virtuous, Wicked
S	*Typology 31, the not-checked-out employee.* Departs job function or status by leaving one position to go to another that requires different types of access. For example, as military separate or retire, then check in as a civilian or, a contractor. Because of transition, they could retain system privileges, authorities, distribution lists in lieu of cancellation. Privileged users must be checked out properly from any organization.	Virtuous, Wicked
S	*Typology 32, the laissez-faire trainee.* Bypasses training, doesn't keep up with system-specific training. Doesn't pay attention in training.	Virtuous, Wicked
Core	**B. Organizational Process Risk Factors That Influence or Contribute to the Outcome of Unintended Insider Threat**	**Lead/control (Use as a checkoff sheet to determine if and where this fits in your organization)**
S	*Audit risk factor.* Audit systems should be in place in an organization. This includes conducting physical and cyber audits on a random basis, as well as routine.	

(Continued)

Table 3.1 (*Continued*) Factors That Contribute to Unintended Insider Threat

CATEGORY	CORE CATEGORY = C, OR SUB-CATEGORY = S	LEAD/CONTROL
S	*Sending outside organization's network.* Several risks may be mapped to this including unconfirmed addresses, office, people, proprietary nature of information sent, restrictions on that information, violating protocols.	
S	*Policy risk.* As part of organizational process, policy plays a role in establishing protocols. However, policy may not be followed, or can be perceived as being poor policy and therefore operators may act differently. Policy may instead create perceived roadblocks to inhibit practical operations and may not be enforced organizationally. Additional policy could have other consequences counter to intention.	
S	*Money.* Lack of organizational prioritization or understanding of acceptable risk to adequately prioritize specifically known security risk mitigation measures.	
S	*Training and education.* Training and education may or may not be in place. Training and/or education may not be current enough or adequate for continually emerging changes.	
S	*Chain of custody risk.* Not understanding sensitivity of data in the chain of custody of that data extends from collection to end state of data.	
S	*Management of personnel behavior risk.* Not understanding red flags in personality, disorders, behaviors, and/or changed behaviors in staff.	
S	*Communications risk to senior leadership.* Staffs not being able to present to senior leadership in the right way, or the rules of the cyber world, to restrict it.	
S	*Organizational reputation.* Making the organization look bad, may be internal or external.	
Core	**C. Physical Environmental Risk Factors**	**Lead/control (Use as a checklist to determine if and where this fits in your organization)**
S	*Unprotected equipment.* Physical barriers not always in place or properly used to protect equipment. Especially check locks, and who has the key.	
S	*Internal physical exposure to different agencies and contractors.* Allowing knowledge that extends beyond need-to-know due to physical proximity of work spaces.	
S	*Computer security access.* On-screen access should be limited to authorized viewers/users. Positioning of monitors of cubical constructions.	

(Continued)

Table 3.1 (*Continued*)   Factors That Contribute to Unintended Insider Threat

CATEGORY	CORE CATEGORY = C, OR SUB-CATEGORY = S	LEAD/CONTROL
s	*Illusion of privacy and security.* Illusion of privacy while talking on phone or using other technology.	
s	*Mask of familiar interface.* Familiarity does not mean safe and secure.	
s	*Lack of cyber-physical digital analog bilingualism.* Not understanding how one or the other is different. For example, mailing an email, not the same as sending letter home. Email has extensive repeatability on servers around the world.	
s	*Lack of equipment accountability.* Not keeping proper track of equipment.	
s	*Physical geographic misperceptions.* Thinking in terms of analog geography vice cyber reality; threat doesn't depend on distance.	
Core	**D. Architectural Information Technology System Wellness**	**Lead/control (Use as a checklist to determine if and where this fits in your organization)**
s	*Openness.* Open ports and file transfer protocol. System architecture that allows for open discovery, and not locked down. This means it is not restricted.	
s	*Privileged user.* More access to systems and granted greater permissions within the system to utilize or change the system.	
s	*A basic user with root access.* A user who does not understand high-level permissions and could delete valuable system data and enterprise files unknowingly.	
s	*Role-based access.* System may allow for greater access than is necessary, and unless role-based access is implemented too much access may be granted.	
s	*System-of-sending.* Unsecure, could be visible to others if protections are not used.	
s	*Error propagation through technological facilitation.* An error being repeated due to system set ups, such as reply all or distribution lists that may contain contacts that should not be used because of less secure email addresses.	
s	*Seamless technology.* Technology can appear to be too seamless to understand the risk. People may become too comfortable with systems that are linked together, such as phones, and phone applications with various security levels.	
s	*Enterprise change management.* If not properly engineered, changes could expose the network.	

(*Continued*)

Table 3.1 (*Continued*)   Factors That Contribute to Unintended Insider Threat

CATEGORY	CORE CATEGORY = C, OR SUB-CATEGORY = S	LEAD/CONTROL
Core	**E. Aggravated Risk Mitigation Approach**	**Lead/control (Use as a checklist to determine if and where this fits in your organization)**
s	*Inappropriate or untimely action without needed collaboration.* Rushing to fix a perceived threat could have greater consequence than the threat itself. Coordination may be necessary before taking a system or person offline or performing a mass denial subprogram.	
s	*Mitigating cyber threat without reaching out to physical security management.* Those persons removed from system access could still pose a physical threat; coordination should be planned and required.	
s	*Moving too slowly.* Leaving identified risks open too long to fix a known threat (a balance is needed). Network evaluations may delay fixes.	
Core	**F. The Unknown Factors**	**Lead/control (Use as a checklist to determine if and where this fits in your organization)**
s	*Unknown consequence linkages.* Organizations may not be able to correlate from a single user or other event compromise to a particular outcome or consequence.	
s	*Unknown, but known threats.* Users or management may not be given latest threat information due to a need-to-know basis, or risk of leaking information regarding this vulnerability. Direction to avoid specific risk may be given, but trust is required to comply.	
s	*Unknown disclosures from business.* Disclosures of information may occur from other business sources for individuals or organizations. Difficult to track this without proprietary knowledge planning.	
s	*External storage.* Unknown how many people are storing hard copy or data work products where they should not.	
s	*Already known, but not shared.* Threat may remain unknown to an organization or agency, even though it may have been identified elsewhere.	

Insider threat is a phenomenon that can, in part, be observed empirically with a keen eye, although not always easily observed if people aren't trained to understand what type of behavior they should be seeking. Employees should understand what type of behavior is acceptable and that which is not acceptable. When incidents do arise, they should learn from their best practices. Indeed, individual motives and actions can and should be better understood that mitigation controls can be implemented. Primary examples of factors that contribute to unintended insider threat are presented as follows:

- Human behavioral risk factors as typologies
- Organizational process risk factors
- Physical environmental risk factors
- Architectural IT system wellness risk factors
- Aggravated risk mitigation approach
- Unknown factors

There are several themes of these factors to also consider. Themes that emerged have centered on *human behavior, organizational processes*, and the *physical environment*. Notably, actions that are intended to assist and mitigate risk could also cause additional damage and increase risk and could cause a cascading impact of unintended incidents. A well-coordinated response is a necessity for an organization to minimize additional risk. This includes communication between hierarchical levels, as well as between both traditional and cybersecurity offices. Unknowns, or unshared known information, are also emergent themes as factors contributing to unintended insider threat. Human behavior is a significant contributing factor for increasing risk within an organization. Risky human behavior extends well into the physical domain, beyond the user keyboard. Human behavior has emerged to become the weakest link even while responding to discovered threats. Not only that, but this behavior extends throughout the organization at all levels.

Along with human behavior, the organizational processes that humans have created, or failed to create, in conjunction with the physical environmental risk factors are of a concern. How well a broader architectural computer system is initially designed or subsequently modified is a risk factor that also includes particular assigned users, the privileged, the root based, and those with role-based access.

Even when employees try to do the right thing, such as identify a threat, and take that threat off-line they can still create a situation even worse than the initial threat.

Unknowns are often not just unknowns in the construct of general knowledge, but instead the distribution of that knowledge can be known to some parts of an organization and to a lesser degree in other parts of an organization. This demonstrates a greater need for information sharing and in some cases developing the processes, as well as accountability regimes to be more effective. The next section presents further discussion on the complete findings presented in Table 3.1.

3.2 Human Behavioral Risk Factors as Typologies

The cultural environment of an organization can help us better understand insider threat and influence and/or intervene on how individuals behave (or could potentially behave) in a social psychological context, within the groups that they belong, or interaction within the organization.

Although one mitigation strategy is to identify anomalies in employee behavior in the workplace: such as staying late; downloading or sending large files; or accessing information that is outside of an employee's scope of work. There are many other behaviors contained in the typology listings that can be equally monitored and managed to reduce risk against the organization today. Leads for managing this effort will need to be established. Typically, monitoring is something that an employee needs to be informed about, and that use of organizational equipment allows for detailed monitoring as well. However, monitoring of other behaviors mean that leads responsible need to collaborate on the best practice for this monitoring, as well as ensuring that civil rights and liberties are adhered to.

Typology 1, the *transporter-carrier*. Everyone loses things. I bet you have lost, during your lifetime, your car keys, your purse, your man bag, your credit cards, your orthodontic retainer, and yes—even your identification cards. At some point we have all misplaced or lost something. Some of these lost items go into a mystical land possibly where all the missing socks have gone; you know the land. However, some missing items are very much a threat and they do not simply vanish. These threats increase your risk. If you are a transporter of work documents, either an electronic storage device or hardcopy form, you are living on borrowed time. It is all too common a scenario, placing a bag on the seat beside us while riding metro and the bag gets left behind, or quickly getting out of a hired car and again your bag is left behind. When an employee transports documents to and from work, they are at risk of losing information. Important information. It happens all the time, so don't do it. Despite well-meaning intentions, it only takes the briefest of moments or inattentiveness to lose an employer's intellectual capital or a client's personal information, your life will be forever changed. Common are reports of theft of personal information or proprietary information from unlocked cars, even in the driveways of their owner. Being a transporter or carrier is an increased human behavioral risk. Creating policy that limits what is allowed to be transported is a way to mitigate or minimize this risk. Having random spot-checks of employees leaving the organization, and oversight by those who know what can be removed and what cannot be removed will reinforce policy and help mitigate this risk.

If you are curious, I know I was, the *Uber Lost & Found Index* provides some interesting data on the items most commonly forgotten in their transports.[1] Notably, the most recent index demonstrates that commuters in the morning are less likely to forget, but that the spikes of forgetfulness of commuters increases between the hours of 4:00 p.m. and 7:00 p.m.; among the top 10 items of forgetfulness include bags and backpacks, which in my opinion could easily hold proprietary work products.

Typology 2, the *litterer*. This one is complex and requires extensive inspection of on-site security for periodic inspection of materials. Recycling materials can be attributed to the virtuous person who means well, but may recycle proprietary information that should be crosscut shredded or burned. Those who are leaving out information and/or stepping away temporarily can be monitored through traditional security programs such as unannounced walk-throughs and spot-checks on a random and frequent basis. It is quite difficult to identify those who are intentionally throwing out data to be vengeful or malicious. Having a secure electronic backup, and in some cases, hard copy documents in a secure location will minimize this loss should a need exist to retrieve them. However, ensuring that the supply chain of your trash is secure is equally important.

Spend the time to ensure that trash and recycling bins are periodically and randomly inspected. Ensure that the recycling contract contains provisions that direct periodic inspections of materials and verify that the contractor is not owned or connected to competitors in any way. Your company's security personnel should walk through the entire supply chain of waste management. If there are disposal bins for proprietary information, those bins should also be locked or kept in a secure location and not open for anyone to pick through or pick up sensitive information.

Typology 3, the *too-tolerant being*. A lack of accountability of peers, subordinates, supervisors, contractors, and others leads to this typology risk. An effective policy is key to mitigating the risk of individuals being too tolerant of each others' poor cyber hygiene practices. Of course, there tends to be some discretion left to supervisors, however violations that place the organization at risk, including human behavior, should be addressed and repeat offenders held accountable. Education and communication of policy throughout the organization is also effective in mitigating this risk. Accountability of personnel actions that run contrary to policy should be published in the annual report and used as a deterrent and a constant warning to staff of unacceptable behavior. This also sends a message to the workforce of the importance to adhere to policy.

Typology 4, the *risk revealer*. This risk is an example of those employees who are susceptible to disclosure, being tricked, socially engineered, or shoulder surfed. Almost all of us are susceptible to a certain level of social engineering and remaining alert of new risk areas is increasingly important. Work environments should have a robust social engineering prevention program, which includes training as well as periodic testing of employees' awareness. Pushing out the latest risks to employees can also keep vigilance up. Social engineering has become more specifically targeted, creating opportunities for exploitation over a longer period of time.

Loss associated with social engineering is no joke and can be painfully felt at multiple levels throughout an organization, down to an individual level. The more a threat (perpetrator) knows about an individual, the greater the potential to obtain access into organizations or banking institutions that the unknowing individual uses. Staying on top of the latest scams is important because many of these scams can appear very legitimate. Fools are not the ones being socially engineered, the attempts are on all of us.

Typology 5, the *scattered data collector*. This is the employee that collects information but does not properly password protect it through encryption or password protection. This type of employee may reply to all or send to an email address that is not verified, or pulls the wrong distribution list onto their send list. The supply chain considerations from the collection to the movement and transfer to the end user is not properly secured. If you think in terms of evidentiary process, the chain of custody is disrupted. The information could then go on to be used for other means. Consider if you have ever sent or received an email that was not intended for you. Consider if it was a one-to-one case or if you were on a massive distribution list, which could not be recalled. Even if it can be recalled, within seconds a misguided email may be read, forwarded, and is now repeatable throughout the world. Mistakes can be made. When it is a very important email containing proprietary or private personal information, this can be especially devastating and the risk of liability or loss very realistic and sometimes not quantifiable for years.

Typology 6, the *seldom unexpected*. Individuals who do not alter their behavior and are predictable allow others to be familiar. This is part of basic security knowledge. The more an individual's pattern remains the same, the more predictable their behavior is to those who wish to compromise or infiltrate that pattern. Altering routines so they are not completely predictable may deter, in part, efforts to compromise an individual or area.

An example of how technology can take this to a high level of risk: In November 2017, a global heat map containing accumulated data points from the preceding two years of fitness trackers was published on the internet to highlight usage of the GPS technology. Whereas city centers showed mostly solid light, this was not the case in more remote areas around the globe where fitness trackers were being used by U.S. military personnel during routine physical fitness activity. For example, the posting of this global heat map, a conglomerate of information, remained unnoticed by the military community until Australian student Nathan Ruser[2] stumbled upon it. Ruser tweeted the following statement: "It looks very pretty, but not amazing for Op-Sec. U.S. bases are clearly identifiable and mappable (sic)"

(January 27, 2018). Various observations about this heat map generated a significant amount of chatter that quickly escalated between academics and journalists that swiftly brought together the reveal of what Sly of the *Washington Post* reported on January 29, 2018, summarized as follows: "U.S. soldiers are revealing sensitive and dangerous information by jogging."[3] Indeed, the predictability of a running routine or the typology of seldom unexpected activity on U.S. military bases has been highlighted on a global scale. The availability of this data created additional risk that extended well beyond the U.S. military to include Russia reported Sly. A former British officer Nick Waters[4] tweeted: "Patrol routes, isolated patrol bases, lots of stuff that could be turned into actionable intelligence" (January 28, 2018), and through reasonable deduction goes onto interpret further; "So, using this data, you may theoretically be able to individually identify who was, say, doing laps around the perimeter of a possible CIA black site" (January 28, 2018).

Would altering routine in the middle of the desert made a difference, maybe so? However, knowledge of the potential to track data to create a map is certainly not farfetched. GPS data can be used to track individuals anywhere there is a GPS signal unless that signal is turned off. Monitoring of individuals has reached a very high level, potentially compromising sensitive information to the enemy. Disconnecting these monitoring devices may reduce user ease while simultaneously increasing security and decreasing risk.

Typology 7, the *gluttonous optimizer*. This falls into the category of an individual that is motivated by personal gain. Perhaps not to the level of trying to disrupt or place revenge on an individual or organization, but may simply see the organization as a means to an end.

The gluttonous optimizer is likely to display narcissistic tendencies. Dr. Heitler, a practicing therapist, describes that narcissism creates difficult relationships and may be "redefined as a deficit in *bilateral listening*"[5] and instead hearing primarily their own thoughts and brushing aside the thoughts of others except for when an individual wants to impress someone. Then they can demonstrate an aspect of selective listening in order to impress and be recognized.

Typology 8, the *unknowing curator*. Just because someone is the holder of information, or retainer of knowledge, it does not mean that they have a complete understanding of the use of the knowledge either for its intended purpose or otherwise. Indeed, the curator could be holding information that is the final puzzle piece in a very important puzzle. Release of this knowledge could have cascading impacts and consequences. Also the loss of this information could be equally damaging. The curator could be holding many different parts of a larger puzzle where assembly of all these pieces could be very devastating to an organization's proprietary information.

Typology 9, the *defiant disregarder.* This individual will knowingly violate security practices or training, although their motivations may not be malicious. Working around specific security practices might in fact get the job done, for a boss who is in a rush, or a budget that is not adequately funded. The "yes I can do it" person might fall victim to just too many shortcuts and work-arounds to provide a solution that is less than secure.

Typology 10, the *technically obsolescent.* There needs to be a balance of expertise within an organization where personnel have access to technology refreshes and advances. Investing in the retention of good employees as well as the investment in their training so that they remain current and relevant is very important. It is very easy to underestimate the emphasis in this area. It also means that to remain on the leading edge, experts should attend conferences and panels, as well as read emerging technology literature. When IT communities within an organization are staffed too thinly, then this resource gap or personnel shortage will likely limit opportunity to identify new investments, enhance processes, and reduce risk in information technology security.

Typology 11, the *hygiene-hindered communicator.* Poor receiving and sending hygiene. For example, not ensuring that signature certificates are current and sending to unconfirmed agencies, persons, offices or individuals before verifying the legitimacy of a receiver greatly increases organizational risk. A hygiene hindered communicator may fail to take the time to password protect a document that needs to be protected. Even when there is guidance in place on how to send email, the hygiene hindered will fail to comply by not taking the extra time to verify their work. When snail mail was once the primary means of communications, the majority of correspondence was internally screened for sensitivity before being mailed. Official correspondence was duplicated for hardcopy file retention before the original was routed for postal delivery. Organizations that put into place selected templates may mitigate their risk of rogue messaging; however, this will not protect misdirected mail. Also ensuring that email can be audited could help detect and identify potential high-risk areas.

Typology 12, the *goofing around player*. The best example of this abuse I can provide is someone who sees an open computer, jumps on, and sends an email to themselves or others that is not appropriate, then returns to their own computer responds back to this fake email for record. However, what this demonstrates is that having an unlocked computer terminal can bring about a large number of risks depending on what is stored or managed by that particular employee. Additionally, jokes of a harassing nature could have a counterproductive intent. Goofing around in an office setting with computer technology is simply a bad idea.

Typology 13, the *blissful user*. If employees—computer users—have a lack of awareness and training, they may not be aware of the risks they are creating for the organization. Privileged users, especially if they are socially engineered, might unbeknownst to them allow perpetrator(s) into the network that might stay and observe for some time to better understand the architecture in order to do damage in the future. Blissful is just unaware and is not seeking out an awareness. It can be risky for contractors to be blissful users as well, as less of their work may be subject to internal monitoring if the contractors, or sub-contractors, work off-site.

Typology 14, the *trusted believer*. It is best to be a skeptic when it comes to insider threat. Individuals that take things at face value, or have less-critical thinking ability, might be more prone to social engineering attempts and remain unguarded. It's important to remember that everyone can be tricked or become a social engineering target with even more precision in a spear phishing attempt. Whereas social engineering was once thought to be a trap for fools, perpetrators have created a false sense of security with lures from princes abroad and relatives stuck without money on a vacation gone bad. However, this modus operandi has changed a great deal.

The Federal Bureau of Investigation's Internet Crime Complaint Center (IC3) continues to track the methods used for exploitation; the IC3 recently issued information on the $5 billion dollar scam[6] of email account compromise that targeted businesses working with foreign suppliers and/or businesses that regularly perform wire transfers. Individuals that routinely perform these transfers have been more narrowly targeted. The entry points have varied depending on the attempt that is made toward the individual. The individuals within an organization that have the authority to conduct financial transfers should have additional training on what trust and verify actually means, given specific social engineering attempts. IC3 has identified other forms of email fraud that include promises of romance, unclaimed lottery winnings, employment, and rental scams, all targeting unknowing money mules. Spoofed high-level executive accounts make this easy, as well as attorney impersonations, fraudulent invoice payments, and data theft. Without established intrusion detection systems, emails that appear official in nature may "leak" in and be incorrectly trusted.

Typology 15, the *rushed surge responder*. During surge operations and/or crisis operations, information assurance may decrease leaving gaps between traditional security, such as the physical, and information technology security. External political factors can push an organization into recovering quickly without taking proper precautions to protect or assure information safeguards. Organizations can have responders on retainer, essentially set up to respond to a variety of crisis scenarios, so that the crisis can be better managed without the added pressure of contracting negotiations. The number of crisis is vast but could include a false claim that has gone viral and could jeopardize company trust. Forward planning for an unanticipated crisis is critical. Having technology that can support surge operations that is current, has been updated and is ready to go and is trackable in inventory is also important. Mobile technology in the case of a lawsuit may need to be recalled. What mobile devices are authorized, and which devices are to be used may need to be part of the preplanned surge strategy response plan.

Typology 16, the *memorable password scribe*. Passwords are numerous and can be difficult to remember, and with increasing length and rules for each password type, individuals are prone to write them down. When passwords are written down they have a greater chance of being lost. Remember that previous Uber example: Loss happens everywhere. Also, passwords are more likely to be repeated for different websites, products, or accessibility. Individuals may even email them back to themselves to remember or take pictures of their passcodes. Both work and personal passcodes can be similar and could allow for more accessibility via spear phishing. Maintaining safeguards for passwords, changes, and resets are important to security protocol health. Writing down passwords and keeping that book in the right-hand drawer of your desk is a very bad idea.

Typology 17, the *privileged user abuser.* This particular typology is an example of the ultimate MacGyver, a person who is talented and is a privileged user and is able to create a work-around with permissions. Whereas work-arounds can be of benefit to getting the job done, these work-arounds can also create loopholes where a MacGyver might lower security requirements to stream a pornography movie on their computer, or allow computer gaming, or support other personal interests online that are not authorized.

Typology 18, the *unmonitored teleworker.* This category goes beyond the traditional work productivity at home, and instead goes to information security hygiene at home. It is possible that there can be other members or visitors to a household that should not be aware of what an employee is working on. The same level of security protections may or may not be on an employee's home computer, if that computer is used for professional work could potentially expose the organization's network. If an employee brings a work computer home, there is also the increased risk of theft by leaving equipment in unlocked cars, or the risk of being stolen in a home burglary, for example.

Typology 19, the *wide-open wanderer.* This typology has been touched upon as part of some other behaviors. You know this person, I know you do. It's the person that gets up to go to the bathroom or the printer, and doesn't bother to lock their computer, leaving it open for anyone to log into. This can happen at any level of the organization, from entry level to executive level. I've seen this happen even at service organizations where I know there is a lot of personal information stored. Employees should immediately lock their computers when they get up from their desks, no exceptions, no excuses, and period.

Typology 20, the *verbal space cadet.* Oh boy, how I love to hate this particular typology. I have seen this typology increasing in recent years, especially when some mobile devices now require special adaptors for privacy headsets. For whatever reason, many conversations are now being placed on speakerphone in open places with increased volume. Not so smart. Many topics of conversation are not private anymore because of this verbal space cadet. Ok, so I'm guilty of start-ing to engage in some conversation when the phone is on speaker, just to raise the awareness of the mobile user. It usually meets with nega-tive looks. Those who use the speaker phone that ignore their physical surroundings and are not aware of what personal information they are disclosing, while the individual on the other line has no idea they are surrounded by strangers in their conversation, places everyone at risk. Information that needs to be protected is especially at risk. In the office environment which is tragically set up with modular cubicle furniture, despite the best acoustic set up, is still at risk. It is best to think about what personnel need to be assigned to offices, what team rooms there are, and what protocols are in place for discussing specific information, a when and where. As an exercise if you spent just one day listening actively in the space around you, throughout the day, you are likely to identify potential threats and even actual cases of increased risk.

Typology 21, the *unguarded doorman*. This typology might be viewed as a not-my-problem character. For example, the credentials should be checked for the technician that is reviewing the cables in your closet or upgrading particular software in-person. There are entry points into networks and if unguarded, intrusions are more likely to occur. If an individual wants to take virtual control of a computer in order to fix a problem, and the unguarded doorman authorizes this work without checking legitimacy and credentials, this poses an increased insider threat.

Typology 22, the *absentminded*. This typology is worth discussion because it is about the absentminded, perhaps the good employee that might seemingly forget, and it's a one-off thing. Stress can lead to for-getfulness as well. It's important to require vigilance of all employees, and if some employees start to deteriorate in this capacity, it might be time to retrain or assess the employee–employer relationship. Medical situations can emerge that might create this type of circumstance. Situations like this do occur in both the private and public sectors. For example, performance may deteriorate because of accidental injury on the one hand, and decrease mental alertness from dementia or another medical condition that might require medication that brings on fatigue or mental fog on the other.

When an unfortunate situation like this emerges, individuals should be assessed for readiness and level of position. A position may need to be adjusted or shifted into a function with minimal risk and increased supervision. Adherence to Civil Rights law needs to take place so ensuring that action is taken that meets legal requirements is equally important.

Typology 23, the *face-off subordinate*. Who hasn't observed this once in their careers, right? The face-off subordinate is about those employees that do not like their supervisors and do not make life easy for their supervisors who look out for their best interests, essentially outright sabotage or withholding vital information. The subordinate may still be true to their perception of ethics and a love for the organization, but are unable to really view their behavior in terms of not being able to see the forest for the trees. Employees that are toxic to their supervisors are also being toxic to their organizations (and not to say it doesn't work the other way around—it does); however, an employee may not realize how their actions are sabotaging the work environment, larger unit, organization, or bottom line.

Typology 24, the *shortcut alleyway takers*. This one is fairly straightforward; those who want to take the shortcut and be on easy street are at a higher threat level to the organization. The easy way could be the least expensive way for technology reinvestment or easier yet, outsourcing a problem without fully understanding it. Neither of these options are optimal solutions as each poses a higher threat level to the organization. There are many contracting examples of taking the easy street and being stuck with a much larger bill, or even outdated technology when all was said and done.

Typology 25, the *uninstructed newbie*. If an individual is not familiar with a particular system or process, they may place an organization at risk without realizing it. Using technology without the proper training is a risk. At a simpler level, if an employee does not have basic cybersecurity training before being given access to a computer network, risks could be introduced. For example, if specific sites are not blocked, and an employee accesses personal email, there is a higher risk of creating an entry point for malicious activity to the network from the outside.

Typology 26, the *surprising superhuman*. Listening to other people's conversations is a form of active listening. In a modern-day work environment, office space is often at a premium for business expenditure. There are many employees in open-concept systems that have learned to tune out conversations in order to focus on their work. Whereas there are others that instead pay attention to what their co-workers are saying around them. Even the whispers. Some employees may or may not even try to listen, but the environment is too open and inappropriately transparent. Without making a significant effort, a lot of information can be gleaned simply by entering into an active listening mode. Even staying in a stationary location, the conversations often simply walk by the desk, chair, or position of the employee. An active listener does not need to wander around. These conversations will go to the active listener. Many years ago, as a teen, when I studied at the American Conservatory Theatre in San Francisco, one of the acting exercises was to go into the neighboring park and listen to conversations. After listening to various conversations for about an hour, the goal was to select a conversation and perform an improvisation of what was said. The results were hilarious. The variations of conversations that were acted out and the diversity of information gleaned in one hour were quite interesting. Unfortunately for business, the results of this insider threat are less than funny. Even without electronic listening devices or recordings, the surprising superhuman as an active listener can be an insider threat by knowing or sharing information with others which they should not know about.

Typology 27, the *ivory towered*. Those who are elite, or more specifically, internalize their position status as elite or privileged without full regard to security protocol within an organization are a risk to the organization that should not be ignored. This can be difficult when those who must hold the ivory towered accountable are in a position that is subordinate. Elevating the importance of security and cybersecurity compliance to the ivory towered is a difficult task at best, but it must be done in order to mitigate this risk. I assess that had the strength of the security office been elevated higher in the State Department while Hillary Clinton was the U.S. Secretary of State, she could have gone on to become the 45th U.S. president. Sadly, for Hillary Clinton as a presidential hopeful, and as the Democrats' primary nominee for president, her complete disregard for security hygiene gave the opposition plenty to work with, and public opinion on this topic was decidedly against her. Should the security offices have been monitoring her practices and requiring compliance? I would assess they should have. To a certain extent her employees showed wicked insider threat behavior. Organizing traditional and cybersecurity at a higher level within an organization can assist those in the ivory tower to better comprehend their exposure to risk to then decide just how much risk they are willing to accept, on behalf of not just the organization or business, but at the potential demise of their own careers.

Typology 28, the *road traveler*. A business traveler or tourist of the world may accidentally introduce threat into their computers and mobile devices which can have a cascading impact into a more expansive network once they have returned to their office or home. Business owners will often provide free public Wi-Fi as a service to their customers and as a means to draw more customers into their stores. These convenient Wi-Fi connections are often referred to as hotspots and their presence has exploded in numbers globally during the last decade. Although this sounds great, the reality is that the privacy and security of these open hotspots is extremely weak and at high risk to compromise. Names of these legitimate hotspots can be modified just slightly, so that unsuspecting road travelers are really entering the internet through a malicious hotspot that will track their every key stroke and mouse click or tap.[7] In contrast, the legitimate hotspots provided by business owners will most likely be lacking of encryption, be more susceptible to software vulnerability and be more open for eves dropping, often called snooping and sniffing or a man-in-the-middle attack where transmissions are basically run through a reader for a third party to review.[8]

Businesses can establish Virtual Private Networks (VPNs) for their employees to mitigate this risk. There are various software companies that can facilitate investment in this technology. Additionally, having technical support available to guide employees through the complex settings of their devices to minimize risk while traveling, is important to maintaining good security protocol. Many popular tourist attractions are also popular virtual pickpocket destinations. From a personal risk standpoint, never visit financial websites that contain your financial information from these Wi-Fi hotspots. Simply browsing for the fun of it or posting updates for social media should be avoided when a secure network is not available. Fun pictures will look just as fun if there is a delay in posting and a Wi-Fi hotspot is the only means for posting.

Typology 29, the *part-present part-timer*. This could easily be a full-time employee who has their mind elsewhere and believes that they are conducting other work of greater importance or value outside of the work environment. A part-time employee who is also relying on more substantive work in another organization could be focusing on a larger payday elsewhere. The back and forth of information between work accounts to private accounts should be avoided—at minimum monitored, as well as potential misuse of proprietary business property.

Entrepreneurs can easily have multiple ventures underway, but ensuring that there is a clear delineation that does not violate policy or ethics, and what the lawyers call a *Chinese wall*, where the conflicts of interest shall not meet. Proprietary information could easily be syphoned away from the primary organization. Greed can factor into this, but also not paying an employee enough money to sustain themselves where they must have two and three part-time jobs or ventures can create a risky situation. Is there an organizational policy on the types of work that can be conducted outside the organization? What type of non-disclosure agreements should be in place? These are questions that should be addressed periodically.

A part-time employee might not invest enough time, or be allotted enough time to understand organizational protocol, procedures, policies that ward off insider threat, or realize they are part of the equation. A part-time employee might more easily dismiss rules because they are not invested as a full-time employee.

Typology 30, the *storyteller, too-busy-to-tell*. There are many lessons learned within an organization, some stories need to be scoped and should be shared. There can be resistance from disclosing what is perceived to be a negative. However, some could be more strategically shared so that the reputation of the organization and individuals is not damaged, but the lesson is ingrained into the culture. Opportunities for success can be created through organizational storytelling. Traditional security and cybersecurity professionals are, for the most part, not used to storytelling within their organization, and unfortunately mistakes are often repeated. Individual accountability is important, but sharing these lessons learned and best practices through creative storytelling can last and shape a culture.

Typology 31, the *not-checked-out employee*. Today's worker is much more portable, and their role may become interchangeable within a particular industry, even within the same organization. If an employee changes roles, divisions, functions, or converts to a contract employee, keen attention should be placed on the individual's privileges and accessibility. If levels of access are no longer required to access particular parts of an organization, either through traditional security or cybersecurity, then these privileges should be adjusted or eliminated. I once observed a former executive of an organization acting in a different role as an entrepreneur in an attempt to obtain proprietary information from a junior member of the organization. While this junior member held up to the pressure, I'm sure that it would only be a matter of time for the former senior executive to get the information sought from someone who perhaps would not hold up as well.

Recently, I was visited by a former employee who had gone through the chameleon change and I wanted to expand on some of the progress I had accomplished as well as recently discovered risks. However, because I knew this person's role had changed, I had to edit my dialog and pay very close attention and choose my words carefully. Without this conscious effort, I could have disclosed information that was not intended for the audience.

Typology 32, the *laissez-faire trainee*. All employees in this modern era need both traditional and cybersecurity training. Without monitoring and accountability of training completion, and testing and evaluation, the benefit of training can be marginal if an employee does not understand fully the reason for this training or does not absorb the materials. Memorization without more complex understanding and pragmatic application leaves a higher risk to an organization. In some law enforcement agencies, a letter with police officer acknowledgment is placed into the officer's record upon completion of training. This places a certain amount of personal accountability on the officer when operating within the line of duty. As cities and states often bear the financial burden of errors in the field, this accountability demonstrates their diligence. If the police officer does not properly follow policy, especially in more extreme cases of disregard, the accountability and liability could shift to individual police officer as an individual and not covered under the scope of the city or state.

While these are 32 typologies presently identified, as time progresses, more behavior typologies may start to emerge. Training that once provided support, including on-the-job training, may gradually disappear as more individuals work in different ways. If organizations use less employees and more contract support, the risks can also change or shift, especially if the work is performed off-site.

It's impossible to predict the future. The projections for combat and for security were quite different at the turn of the millennium than they turned out to be. The global war on terrorism changed the approach to global security and as a result the world changed its strategies and resultant cascading policies, regulations, and enforcement methods. The United States underwent a massive federal reorganization, the largest since WWII, in which the U.S. Department of Homeland Security was formed.[9] Women became accepted in traditionally filled male combat roles. Several of the transportation systems sector modes of transportation had to change their security approaches significantly. The awareness of threats in cybersecurity have gradually increased, but there is a lot more understanding that needs to be gained for protection against these threats. Insider threat is one of these cybersecurity threats, and there has been less awareness of these threats. The 32 typologies of human behavior are an example of very specific actions where action can be taken to mitigate these risks.

Twenty years in the future, what will the workplace look like? Technology applications are increasingly changing. Even today, a seemingly harmless application may carry with it higher levels of risk; for example, the fitness tracker when geographically placed on a global display. Showcasing how workers seemingly born with a smartphone in their right hand are more likely to feel comfortable with using this technology while not likely fully understanding its risks. Technology has become so integrated that the connection aspects, even to technological administrators, have become increasingly abstract.

3.3 Organizational Process Risk Factors

Processes within an organization should be known and clearly understood by those who must operate within them. This seems simple enough, but it is not always the case. As time marches on and employees rotate in and out, and new policies supersede older policies, the understanding of processes in organizations can become increasingly murky. If training does not take place to explain these changes and follow on measurement and accountability is absent, insider threat will greatly increase. However, not all of these typologies can be mitigated through computer settings. Validation and verification are often needed ranging from audit controls to human verification of information. Policies and procedures should be in place and adapted, based on assessments, in order to mitigate risk. Reaching out to employees on a regular basis will be important to ensure they understand these communications and that a trusted relationship is fostered and developed. For example, if computers have standardized configurations, organizations can change logon screens to reflect areas of cybersecurity emphasis. Employees should feel that their observations will be taken seriously. Monitoring is important. Agreement, or better yet, a reminder of monitoring and compliance with policy can also be placed on these initial login screens.

The larger the organization, the more complex these processes become in practice. Processes can also be informally changed by managers directing changes to these processes, but without the proper updated guidance, risk is introduced to the process which quickly increases misalignment. Insider threat, the virtuous, wicked, vengeful, and malicious, can breed in these types of murky environments.

Various processes should be considered to counter insider threat. The following is not an all-inclusive list, but it's a good start: audit; external communication outside the organization's network; policy health; prioritization of investment as related to risk; training and education; chain of custody; management of behavior risk; communications of risk to senior leadership; and organizational reputation considerations.

Audit systems should be in place in an organization. This includes conducting audits of traditional security as well as cyber-related audits on a random and routine basis. Organizational leadership should ensure that audits are a catalyst for organizational change and should follow through and monitor those changes. Audits can be conducted internally or by external sources. There are many industry standards and benchmarks to measure against, depending on the process or system being audited. Without audit systems in place, unchecked errors will perpetuate the insider threat.

Sending data outside the organization's network becomes an issue when the information either arrives at the wrong destination or the content that is being released outside the organization violates policy, both perpetuate the insider threat. It is more difficult to assess that information has been lost in this way.

As part of the organizational process, policy plays an important role in establishing practice; however, if some of these policies are perceived to be too difficult, and there is not sound enforcement and accountability, work-arounds are bound to quickly emerge.

Investment in the correct organizational prioritization against insider threat is not always determined at budget boards. Competing demands may take priority. Although the workforce is becoming savvier about insider threat, a knowledge gap remains in cybersecurity. Even with the prioritization of increased training and education, the exploitations of and through information technology systems continue to grow. Real-time awareness needs to be pushed on an ongoing basis. Loss of sensitive data resulting from poor chain of custody hygiene greatly increases insider risk.

Without impeding on civil liberties, organizations should know their employees. When personnel behaviors start to change, managers are in a position to refer employees to employee assistance programs, or security managers, depending on the nature of the change. Throughout an individual's career, it should be expected that there are ups and downs in each person's life. However, some of the downs could leave an employee more vulnerable to being socially engineered, or susceptible to bribery, or even engaging in other vengeful or malicious activities against their organization. Both traditional security and cybersecurity risk should be looked at. Incidents of workplace violence and active shooter situations could emerge from behavior that should be red flagged. Even domestic situations could escalate into workplace violence. According to the Census of Fatal Occupational Injuries, nearly 2 million American workers have reported being a victim of workplace violence and statistics show that reported deaths in the U.S. workplace also continue to increase.[10] Workplace homicides increased to 500 deaths in 2016, as did workplace suicide to 291 deaths, the highest figures since 2010 in homicide and the most suicides since reporting began in 1992.[11] Protective service occupations increased by 68 fatalities to 281 deaths, an increase of 32 percent.

On April 12, 2012, James Wells, a disgruntled U.S. Coast Guard civilian employee shot and killed two co-workers, firing multiple times with a .44-caliber weapon at his place of employment at the U.S. Coast Guard Communications Station Kodiak, Alaska. It was posited that after increased supervisory oversight was placed on him and was denied travel orders to attend a national conference as a subject matter expert on antennas, that he committed this heinous crime. It was a conference that he had typically attended each year and it was deduced that the escalation and planning of killing his colleagues had started as a result of his perceived exclusion.

Although James Wells did not testify during his trial, he maintained his innocence. The evidence convicting him was convincing, including finding matching .44-caliber rounds in his home, establishing access to a weapon (that was never recovered), a flawed cover-up story that pointed to fake telephone voicemails to both victims in the office, and a self-inflicted nail into his tire as a cover story. He was convicted beyond a reasonable doubt of killing retired U.S. Coast Guard Chief Boatswain's Mate Richard Belisle, and U.S. Coast Guard Petty Officer First Class James Hopkins. Wells was sentenced to the maximum of four consecutive life sentences and is presently serving his sentence in a federal prison in Colorado. However, in December of 2017, the 9th Circuit Court of Appeals granted Wells the right to a retrial. A panel of judges ruled that prosecutors repeatedly overstepped their boundaries including using an expert witness in workplace violence; a new trial has been ordered, though Wells remains incarcerated pending trial outcome.[12]

Workplace incidents are not without other consequences, such as reputation and liability. As summarized by Wireless Estimator (which publishes an industry related communications news blog), the spouses of Belisle and Hopkins in 2016 sued the U.S. Coast Guard under the Federal Tort Claims Act asserting that the organization should have known James Wells was disgruntled, dangerous, and out of control citing the evidence of numerous reprimands and disciplinary sanctions.[13] When an incident occurs that causes loss of life, and in this case homicide, it is human resources records that can be looked back upon to determine if there were opportunities to identify the threat earlier, and to take steps to identify behavioral issues to minimize the potential for a crime of this nature.

Damages created through cyberspace can have consequences that are financially damaging as well as potentially creating a physical threat that could lead to death. A SCADA system, a pathway to be able to communicate a potential increased risk to senior managers and/or executives should be available. If security is a lower priority in an organization and not immediately available in a crisis then security delays can be costly. The perception that risks in traditional and cyber-security along with perceived potential for insider threat exist within an organization, an organizational reputation can be easily damaged. If good employees perceive that an organization is no longer a good option, they may look to transport their careers elsewhere.

3.4 Physical Environmental Risk Factors

Traditional security, including physical security needs to be considered in terms of the role it plays in cybersecurity and insider threat. Illusions of privacy and security are rampant. Newer buildings with office cubicle spacing can have even less privacy and security with potentially alarming open access. Physical barriers may not always be in place properly. For example, if a locked cabinet is in place to secure a server, but the doors remain open, then physical access to cyber connections is accessible with ease. These connections need to be guarded. Wiring in buildings runs through walls and can be contained in specific closets designed to house connections. However, these spaces could double as storage, or janitorial supply closets, leaving them open and exposed shows a potential threat. These types of spaces may not be under surveillance as are larger areas such as main passageways and security checkpoints. Additionally, if storage containers for materials, proprietary or otherwise, are subpar, this will also expose an organization to vulnerability.

Some observant employees pay attention and often know where the gaps in security are and may be willing to share these vulnerabilities if asked directly. For example, I frequently see workers in various employment settings such as fast-food chains and other retail settings huddling in the blind spots of security cameras to access their phones and reach their social media network. Probably because I tend to look at security problems, I may ask workers questions they really shouldn't answer—and surprisingly, employees will share with me the vulnerabilities of their security systems.

Unprotected equipment, especially computer and mobile technology that can get access or allow access into a network is a risk. Open terminals allow a passersby to download files or upload any number of malicious malware. Discussing progress of programs or projects within the close proximity to those who do not need to know should be minimized. The placement of screen views should be considered. In a workplace that feels comfortable, it can become easy to slide into complacency, to not pay attention to who is walking by, who is keeping track, or not keeping track of computer equipment. It's easy to forget that distance in cybersecurity does not matter. An internet connection thousands of miles away is closer than walking across a room to open the door. Once information is sent, it may route through a server that is repeatable throughout the world, in mere fractions of a second.

3.5 Architectural IT System Wellness Risk Factors

Discovery of wellness risk factors of an information technology system may require both a remote and physical validation and audit. Even if policies and rules are in place, the common organizational practice needs to be clearly identified. If you are in an organization with a distributed workforce, with locations in multiple areas, it is likely that consistency of your infrastructure could vary. The openness of systems needs to be examined, as well as validating the people that should have access to these systems, and the identification of those individuals that really should not have access. Many organizations will lock down computer ports when terminals are unplugged, reactivating them when someone is authorized to connect. This takes additional time but can minimize the risk of unauthorized access into a network. As discussed, simply connecting a mobile device into a computer to charge the battery creates a connection that can allow for the transfer of data and a doorway will open. Ports should be labeled, or excess ports be blocked as a precautionary measure.

Individuals that are given increased privileges or access should be scaled and actively managed. Vetting and regular revalidation of the need should occur. For example, if someone only needs high-level access once a year to submit a report, they should probably not retain the access all year long. It is just not good security practice to do so. This access should be provided for a very short period to submit the report and then be closed. In some cases individuals are given proxies to do work, and these proxies should be used on a case-by-case basis and not be retained. Individuals that transfer positions within an organization could be a risk for the organization if they continue to carry the accessibility controls and are tempted to either use them or are complacent allowing someone else to access. I witnessed the spouse of a worker a few years ago accessing an application from home in order to change some personnel data, in a web-based system—a system that she should not have been authorized to use or navigate in. She navigated the system with ease, and this surprised me.

While the data changes were ultimately authorized, the spouse did not have organizational permission to be in the system; the credentials of the worker could have been used to perform other changes and view other information had they gone to different viewing screens. Without more advanced biometrics, this might have been difficult to detect, since the two factor authentication credentials were present in order to access the system.

When a user has root access, a lot of damage can be done because the user has elevated privileges that can delete and move around infrastructure. If a malicious threat is in your network, deleting may not be the aim, and instead the aim may be to gather as much information as possible. Terrorists and malicious users are not always in the game to destroy, but to collect. With root access, once inside the network, they can easily hide for months because they would have used those credentials to build authorized and legitimate places to hide. This can be very difficult to detect and explains why some companies release breaches well past their expiration dates, or the breaches become increasingly vast than initial reports. Computer forensics can be difficult to achieve.

Technology that is seamless can also cause problems. The future workforce will likely rely more on technology and will have increasingly technology habits (good or bad) that they bring with them from home and college into the workplace. These practices not necessarily cybersecure, which place organizations at greater risk. Quite frankly these changes can be difficult to keep up with. Their patterns and weaknesses may be more predictable, as the latest technology seems to really be attractive to trying. Technology applications are continually changing; a seemingly harmless application may carry with it higher levels of risk. Workers who have been born with technology in their hands are more likely to feel comfortable with using this technology, and not likely to fully understand the risks of it because it is seamless. Technology has become so integrated that the connection aspects, even to technical administrative workers has become increasingly abstract.

3.6 Aggravated Risk Mitigation Approach

It is important to not make the situation worse, and therefore a plan is needed. Without a plan to respond to an elevated threat against a traditional security or cybersecurity incident, you could be making your situation even worse. You can soon find yourself responding to alarms where you may not be able to determine if you have a real insider threat or if you are dealing with nuisance alarms. Meaning you can't see the forest for the trees, especially if you do not know what your network looks like, or who is connected to your network at any given time. These shorter term and often false alarms can be distractions from a bigger issue that needs a larger organizational change action. For example, if you have an intrusion, it is possible that the intrusion is not a critical one and taking swift action could interfere with critical operations.

However, there may be other approaches to determine the level of the threat, and to determine who is in the system, how they got in the system, and why and/or how the intended breach originally occurred. For example, assessing if the attack was deliberate and targeted, or random and/or serious, or a nuisance, all should be a priority. The scope of the compromise will need to be determined as well. It might be possible to isolate the breach without alerting the intruder to prevent further compromise before disconnecting. It might be possible to place some false information before closing the door. Some very good technical experts are needed for this counter-operations practice.

Marketing and damage control are very important. Mapping accountability chains will also be important. If an investment was not taken to save money, but the intrusion cost the organization more than the original mitigation measure, this should be known for future investments. Making a problem worse through a haphazard response approach is not ideal, and this approach should be avoided. If the network and technology connections are monitored, and a threat is identified, understanding exactly how the network is mapped will be very important to isolating a threat. If a large intrusion has been identified, the gut reaction might be to launch a full response. However, a quick pause to come up with a course of action is recommended; or a pre-established course of action that makes sense could be implemented; in either case, the response should not cause larger consequences. It can be both a deductive and inductive process depending on the multitude of issues. Combining both traditional and cybersecurity assessments will be needed. Because technology is not always in the clouds, and there are physical connections, these connections need to be audited and/or verified. Understanding if a connection is isolated and whether there will be secondary impacts to an even more critical system will be important to know. There may be multiple solutions, involving various mitigation techniques, and the more that is known the better so that risk can be reduced with the best approach. If your network is not mapped, that is a very good place to start. From an information technology perspective, it will be very important to have mapped your network so that you can isolate potential risk areas if needed. A physical inventory along with updating the latest anti-virus protection is important. Also, if your employees connect straight to the internet and are using standalone computers, you should know what networks your employees connect to. So, how well is the information that they are storing for you or the proprietary information of your/their clients, protected?

In the physical world if an environment is not safe, it can often be assessed through a boots-on-the-ground approach. Assessing everyone, from the lowest level employees to the most senior, including contractors and other personnel, with connections. The insider threat response needs to employ dual approaches. If there are domains on the network that should be removed, or old software that pose a risk, or out-of-date operating systems, these should have been identified and removed in advance. However, responses to situations can in hindsight bring these types of mitigation strategies to light—typically and unfortunately, later than they should have been.

If the operator of a computer terminal, through their risky behavior, created the open doorway and was indeed part of this insider threat, then on-the-spot remediation training will be needed with the individual, or other predetermined course of action. Accountability remains important. Taking this lesson learned and knowledge to determine if the same issues are occurring more broadly with other computer users on multiple terminals will be as equally important.

3.7 Unknown Factors

Recognizing that we can't know everything is important because factoring in unknown risk is critical to recovery. Individuals and their organizations may be trying to make the right decisions but with limited visibility. The unknown is always a risk, because you don't always know what you don't know. Even after an incident, gathering a chain of events leading to a casualty can be a challenge. Supply chain sources can be questionable even if an organization has a trusted source, the threat of a product may change relatively quickly, leaving a security gap. To have a high level of confidence, an entire supply chain must be verifiable; from the manufacturer to transportation to the validated vendor that sells the part to the installer.

I took a systems thinking course with a very dynamic group of federal aviation administrators at the Department of Transportation's Center of Excellence several years ago. Collectively, we explored taking a "systems thinking approach" in order to reduce some of the blinders or ideological perceptions. What we discovered is that there are a lot of perception risk areas. This course I think was a catalyst for me in researching the concepts of thinking critically.

3.8 Practical Mental Models Continued

As discussed, mental models are beneficial for conceptualization of complex topics. A more comprehensive understanding of insider threat should begin to emerge. I continue to unfold the 10 mental models that are all aspects of a grounded theory of insider cyber threat. Building on the prior two mental models—*Aspect 1: At the Crossroads* and *Aspect 2: The Virtuous and the Wicked*—I will now introduce two more. The chapter will continue to build your understanding of this definition and conceptualization with very practical application. The creation of a new understanding of insider cybersecurity threat to an organization is being revealed to you.

3.8.1 Mental Model (Aspect 3)—Risky Human Behavior as Typologies

The next mental model I call *Aspect 3*, which is *a grounded theory aspect of risk factors and unintended insider threat; 32 human behavioral risk typologies*. To capture the human risk behavior emerging from the data, typologies of human risk were grouped to illustrate groupings of organizational human behavior. Risky human behavioral actions were captured, written into more general categories, and organized into typologies that actually create mental models. These mental models contribute to an organizational understanding of unintended insider threat. These specific 32 typologies that are factors of insider threat may also stand alone as mental models as their descriptive name indicates; however, for discussion purposes, I have captured them categorically.

Table 3.1, specifically Core Category *A*, includes a brief description for each typology as a mental model. This may provide insight and potential opportunity to determine applicability for an organization. Some of the behavior's intent may be inherently clear, while other reasons will need to be later explored by an organization in greater depth so that organizational training or policy changes are addressed in a specific organizational environment. Ultimately, the *Mental Model (Aspect 3)—Risky Human Behavior* may be drastically mitigated with a goal of vulnerability elimination. In essence, through the creation of mental models, what I have captured is storytelling, a risky behavior folded into human caricatured typologies that espouse the reality of insider threat created by both human action and inaction.

This is a great place to begin your organizational assessment and determine your risk by comparing the table against your existing approach and identifying any gaps or deltas. There is opportunity in identifying potential high-risk areas and reducing this risk through systematic remediation. Risk can be reduced by minimizing the number of risk-behavior typologies in an organization. Awareness of these behaviors is a foundational start for an organization to examine, along with creating opportunities to seek ways to shift behaviors to mitigate risk. Every employee, including those not typically considered an employee, can create a vulnerability that introduces this threat and elevates risk. The virtuous, wicked, vengeful, and malicious employees all create risk, of varying consequential magnitude, which may not be initially known. The conceptual understanding of well-intended behavior that can also lead to an accident or an unintended consequence is also necessary. This shift of understanding may lift a potential ideological veil for many organizations.

3.8.2 Mental Model (Aspect 4)—The Enforcer and the Responder

The next mental model, I call *Aspect 4*, is *a grounded theory aspect of an unintended insider threat phenomenon of the enforcer and unchecked risk mitigation countermeasure response.* Risk mitigation efforts were shown to be risky, as captured in typology 15, the rushed surge responder, when actions were perceived as inappropriate or untimely without needed collaboration. Cyber threat often requires the support of traditional security, including physical security, especially when dealing with a human entity. Simply shutting down a person's access may not mitigate additional risk that could be created through a physical presence. However, there was also an identified risk of moving too slowly, and that a balanced and coordinated approach was needed to respond to threats. Not to just respond to either the cyber aspect or the physical aspect, but to also be able to assess the threat and manage the response in a more comprehensive and collaborative way between information technology and physical security.

3.8.3 In Review

This chapter has provided a lot of valuable information on insider threat: assessment and mitigation of risks. It answers the question, what are the factors of insider threats to organization, in a readable and pragmatic way. Much of the information presented provided clues into the unintended insider threat, specifically the virtuous and the wicked, and at times the vengeful and malicious insider. As discussed, key organizational themes emerged on human behavior, organizational process, and the physical environment. Notably, action that was well intended to assist and mitigate risk could also cause additional damage, increase risk, and cause cascading impacts of unintended incidents. A well-coordinated response is necessary for an organization to manage this risk. To do so, additional communications and strategic risk communications between hierarchical levels are required. Unknowns, or unshared known information, were emergent themes and contributing factors to insider threat. Primary examples of factors that contribute to unintended insider threat were presented:

- Human behavioral risk factors as typologies
- Organizational process risk factors
- Physical environmental risk factors
- Architectural IT system wellness risk factors
- Aggravated risk mitigation approach
- Unknown factors

As you may have now identified, with a greater depth, human behavior is a significant contributing factor for increasing the risk within an organization. Insider threat created through risky human behavior impacts cybersecurity and extends well into the physical domain. Along with humans, the organizational processes that humans have created, or failed to create, in conjunction with the physical environmental risk factors are of a concern. How well a broader architectural computer system is initially designed or subsequently modified is a risk factor that also includes particular assigned users, the privileged, the root based, and those with role-based access. More attention should be given to this area. The need to collaborate is only getting stronger; even when employees try to do the right thing, such as identify a threat and take the threat off-line, they can still create a situation even worse than the initial threat.

Unknowns are often not just unknowns in the general knowledge sense, but instead can be known to some part of an organization and to a lesser degree in other parts of an organization. This demonstrates a greater need for retaining knowledge, sharing information, and conducting strategic risk communications surrounding the emergent themes presented for insider threat; assessment and mitigation of risks.

Appendix: Best Practice—Practical Knowledge and Practitioner Application

Practical knowledge

- Review the human behavioral risk factors as typologies, there are 32 identified. Ensure you recognize the increased risks that are created through the risky behavior of the unintended insider threat of the virtuous, wicked, and sometimes vengeful.
- Note distinctions between vengeful, and malicious. At times vengeful consequences are unintended, and not recognized, at other times they are intended. Malicious behavior is destructive and harmful but can also have unintended secondary or tertiary impacts. However, the malicious insider typically falls into the intended insider threat category.
- Recognize that in addition to risky employee behavior in organizations there are other risk factors, specifically: organizational process, physical environment, architectural IT system wellness, aggravated risk mitigation, and the unknown factors.
- Reflect on how the use of mental models may be effectively used to both understand the problem of insider threat and communicate the risk as a tool of mitigation.
- Understand how organization leads for countering insider threat needs should be assigned from multidisciplinary perspectives and work together in collaboration under a comprehensive insider threat program that focuses on the entire threat and risk landscape and not just the predominately external malicious insider threat.

Practitioner application

- Specifically review each behavior typology, identify a current countermeasure in place, or lack thereof, to identify your gaps and deltas.
- Review the factors of insider threats against your identified insider cyber threats to organization Core Category checklist (Chapter 2). Include comparative analysis with organizational

leads, co-leads. Assess and identify any organizational gaps, including missing controls and accountability mechanisms.

- In your organization, assess any recently discovered insider threat events. Assess if the knowledge was unknown, or known and simply not shared. Determine if this communication pathway has been corrected.
- Identify how much of your organizational technology falls into standard configurations and is routinely scanned and patched; identify how to increase the security of the workforce through upgraded operating systems, and standard configurations.
- Determine who are your network enforcers and responders, and if they are available 24/7.
- Review your organization's traditional and cybersecurity training programs and plan to enhance, including adapting stronger personnel accountability measures, at all levels, against insider threat.
- Be prepared to ensure that the people accepting the risk for the organization have the authority to accept this risk, and understand the risk they are accepting.

Endnotes

1. Uber Newsroom. The 2018 Uber Lost & Found Index. (2018). Retrieved from https://www.uber.com/newsroom/2018-uber-lost-found-index/.
2. Nathan Ruser Tweets. Strava Releases Their Global Heatmap. January 27, 2018. Retrieved from https://twitter.com/Nrg8000/status/957318498102865920.
3. U.S. Soldiers Are Revealing Sensitive and Dangerous Information by Jogging by Liz Sly. January 28, 2018. *Washington Post*. Retrieved from www.washingtonpost.com.
4. Nick Waters Tweets. Big OPSEC and PERSEC Fail. January 27, 2018. Retrieved from https://twitter.com/N_Waters89/status/957323495226167296.
5. Narcissism: A redefinition and case study by Dr. Susan Heitler. 2014. Therapy Help. Retrieved from https://www.therapyhelp.com/narcissism-a-redefinition-and-case-study/.
6. Federal Bureau of Investigations. Public Service Announcement (I-050417-PSA). Business email compromise, email account compromise, the 5 billion dollar scam. May 24, 2017. Retrieved from https://www.ic3.gov/media/2017/170504.aspx.

7. What is public Wi-Fi by Norton™ by Symantec Corporation, 2018. Retrieved from https://us.norton.com/internetsecurity-privacy-risks-of-public-wi-fi.html.

8. Ibid.

9. Public Law 107-296. To establish the Department of Homeland Security, and for other purposes. The Homeland Security Act of 2002. Retrieved from https://www.gpo.gov/fdsys/pkg/PLAW-107publ296/html/PLAW-107publ296.htm.

10. U.S. Department of Labor, Occupational Safety and Health Administration. (2017). Workplace Violence. Retrieved from https://www.osha.gov/SLTC/workplaceviolence/.

11. Bureau of Labor Statistics. (2018). Census of Fatal Occupational Injuries Summary, 2016. Retrieved from https://www.bls.gov/news.release/cfoi.nr0.htm.

12. Appeals court orders new trial in a double murder at Kodiak Coast Guard station by Lisa Demer. December 19, 2017. *Anchorage Daily News*. Retrieved from https://www.adn.com/alaska-news/crime-courts/2017/12/19/appeals-court-orders-new-trial-in-a-double-murder-at-kodiak-coast-guard-station/.

13. Wives of murdered tower techs sue the Coast Guard for wrongful death by Featured News. August 16, 2016. *Wireless Estimator*. Retrieved from http://wirelessestimator.com/articles/2016/wives-of-murdered-tower-techs-sue-the-coast-guard-for-wrongful-death/.

4

How Insider Threat Factors Relate to Vulnerability and Consequence

4.1 Introduction

How insider threat factors relate to vulnerability and consequence is a challenging topic area, but one where additional findings have been identified that will be useful to your organization. By vulnerability I mean that insider threat factors allow for exploitation or susceptibility, creating an event, incident, or occurrence of traditional and cybersecurity; the consequence is the result of this exploitation or susceptibility. A consequence is typically considered a more immediate occurrence, in a cause and effect relationship, I have found this is not necessarily the case.

This consequence delay is prevalent with technology. There is often a time delay of consequences making the cause and effect relationship murky. The vulnerability may have been created but the susceptibility, or open door, may not be discovered until later by a deliberate intruder or random passerby, and the consequence experienced at a later time. In order to mitigate the risk created by vulnerabilities, comprehending the breadth and depth of all identified factors of threat that relate to vulnerability and consequence is extremely important. From the identified insider threat factors, not all vulnerabilities nor their associated consequences will be completely known. However, those vulnerabilities that are known should be assessed along with a deliberate effort to implement a risk mitigation action plan. Action is the key word here, as time is of the essence. The virtuous, wicked, vengeful, and malicious insider threats create vulnerabilities where cascading consequences may very well be felt on multiple levels extending outside the organization to its direct external partners. In this global economy, this includes national and international partners and/or stakeholders. Because of this expansive network of direct and indirect partnerships there are a multitude of complex challenges, as you may have already gathered. There is a problematic process with both enforcement and traceability. The advancement of computer forensics continues to improve, with investigative trails adapting to the illusions or counterintelligence in the reality of the source of the perpetrator. As a result, I believe that accountability is going to increase along with assignment of liability, when applicable, and that both will substantially increase around the globe. Consumers are getting smarter about the risks that organizations are taking with their private and personal information and the conglomeration of their data. Also, interest groups are paying attention.

In this chapter, I provide a narrative response to a question as I did in the preceding chapters that directly answer how the factors previously identified relate to vulnerability and consequence. I then provide a listing of categories that are displayed in Table 4.1; these categories are listed for readability in terms of core categories as well as their sub-categories. Again as in previous chapters, I enter into a more comprehensive discussion. Throughout the discussion, practical application, mental models and best practices are called out. Specifically, the categories may be used by an organization to assess risk and to help develop action plans to mitigate that risk.

How do these factors relate to vulnerability and consequence? The answer is as follows.

4.1.1 The Narrative Response

All insider threat factors, including unintended insider threat factors, are related to risk, vulnerability, and consequence. Physical security is very much interconnected to information technology security, and cyber-physical digital-analog bilingualism is called for. Organizational resilience is connected to understanding factors related to vulnerability and their consequences, along with process related to consequences and risk mitigation measures. Linking awareness, increasing competency, applying mitigation measures, storytelling, and linking performance to evaluations and rewards, may enhance organizational resilience.

4.1.2 The Categorical Response

Now that the narrative has been presented, I will list the categorical results. These categorical results may be used in terms of an assessment to identify the organizational responsibility or lead, and assigned control. Specifically from this table, organizations should determine their level of *knowledge and process* in place as a form to counter the threat and mitigate risk. A more descriptive discussion of each of the core categories follows.

Table 4.1 Factors That Relate to Vulnerability and Consequence

CATEGORY	CORE CATEGORY = C, OR SUB-CATEGORY = S	CONTROL (COUNTER/ MITIGATION)
C	**A. All Factors of Insider Threat Vulnerabilities Relate to Consequence**	**Knowledge and management; ensure process, including auditability and accountability**
Note	*All factors that contribute to unintended insider threat relate* (as presented in Chapter 3, Table 3.1, which includes all typologies as well as emergent themes).	
s	*Leaving unattended what shouldn't be.*	
s	*Good employees conducting work-arounds to bypass pain points creates vulnerability.*	
s	*Breaking evidence chains.*	
s	*Traditional spy.* A human as a medium, accessed first through cyber. The employee may not realize they are being used, or may not know and then may fall subject to exploitation.	
s	*Organizational structure and function are more likely to be indiscriminately released.* Creating vulnerability more subject to exploitation.	
s	*Technologically, every system, network, software.* All have a number of vulnerabilities.	
s	*Threat that exploits the vulnerable human link; personalized spear phishing campaign.* The more specific, the greater likelihood that every human will fall prey to something.	
s	*Being open.* Open is vulnerability.	
s	Finding something open accidentally.	
s	Users not knowing how to deal with threats.	
s	Information collected by adversaries via vulnerability and stored for future use.	

(Continued)

Table 4.1 (*Continued*)   Factors That Relate to Vulnerability and Consequence

CATEGORY	CORE CATEGORY = C, OR SUB-CATEGORY = S	CONTROL (COUNTER/ MITIGATION)
S	A disclosure of information.	
S	Gaining password access.	
S	Creating a fake account to use with less detection.	
S	Gaining access that could lead to another area of consequence.	
S	Blatant vulnerability—individuals consistent in their actions.	
S	Factor of abusive administrator rights.	
S	Factor of complacency.	
S	Factor of not being aware.	
S	Factor of being uneducated.	
S	System set up to default settings.	
S	Could hide more, cause havoc to hide tracks.	
S	Repeatability increases vulnerability and consequence (email, text).	
S	Not holding people accountable.	
S	Being vulnerable to illusions of friendship, social media, and gaming.	
S	Being vulnerable to illusions of security and privacy.	
S	Trying to fix broken technology, no longer supported.	
S	Sending to .com and hitting reply all.	
S	Not having a good understanding of systems.	
S	Being linked together.	
S	Unprotected system, vulnerability allows for various types of computer infection, including spreading viruses.	
S	Social media (where technology and humans meet).	
S	Not understanding generational differences in technology experience (risks at every age group that may be different).	
S	Employee termination not properly managed (i.e., employee is notified prior to accounts being disabled).	
S	Downloading or streaming from an unconfirmed origination source.	
S	Interception of Wi-Fi signals on laptops/mobile devices.	

(*Continued*)

Table 4.1 (*Continued*)   Factors That Relate to Vulnerability and Consequence

CATEGORY	CORE CATEGORY = C, OR SUB-CATEGORY = S	CONTROL (COUNTER/ MITIGATION)
S	Not upgrading to better security.	
S	Not training members.	
S	Users not understanding why things are locked down.	
S	Having backdoors not identified by engineers or programmers.	
S	Not holding personnel accountable because the perception of offender being such a nice guy.	
S	Engineers and programmers not testing or identifying backdoors.	
S	Not knowing the threat.	
S	Not identifying proprietary important information that needs protection.	
Core	**B. Consequences Vary on Multiple Levels May Be Viewed as Either (1) Individual, or (2) Organizational from (a) a local impact to (b) an enterprise level internal impact, and (3) Tertiary, broader external impacts at a (a) national, (b) international, or (c) other external partners**	**Knowledge and management; ensure process, including auditability and accountability**
S	Individual consequences as a punishment for employee violators of information security.	
S	Organizational consequence.	
S	Consequences external to primary organization, secondary, tertiary, and so forth. May be proprietary.	
S	National consequence through release of national security information.	
S	Global consequence.	
S	Actual penetration of systems.	
S	Root kit downloaded allowing for freedom to move laterally in the system initially undetected.	
S	A denial of service.	
S	Infection of machines that spreads.	
S	Gaining access to an unauthorized system, such as financial.	
S	Accountability relates to consequence.	
S	Consequence to the network, the more things exposed.	

(*Continued*)

Table 4.1 (*Continued*)   Factors That Relate to Vulnerability and Consequence

CATEGORY	CORE CATEGORY = C, OR SUB-CATEGORY = S	CONTROL (COUNTER/ MITIGATION)
S	Repeatability increases vulnerability and consequence (email, text).	
S	Both intended and unintended factors have consequence.	
S	Cloud compromise can be difficult to track to cascading compromise.	
S	Launching unintended code.	
S	System admin compromise.	
S	Cost related to forensic investigation.	
S	Widespread prohibition from particular systems.	
Core	**C. Problematic Processes Related to Consequences**	**Knowledge and management; ensure process, including auditability and accountability**
S	Problem of consequence is enforcement.	
S	Vulnerability to networks, have to trace back to consequences.	
S	System of self-reporting, ethics, or incentive.	
S	Not being aware of cascading consequences.	
S	Ongoing process to identify and create mitigation measures.	
Core	**D. Other Considerations of Mitigation**	**Knowledge and management; ensure process, including auditability and accountability**
S	People should be challenged to change behavior.	
S	People who reuse patterns; systems could prevent this.	
S	System of self-reporting, ethical appeal, or other incentive.	
S	Set up system defaults to minimize vulnerability for users (reply all, email defaults, sending to .com).	
S	Violations, tiered levels of consequences including training, revocation scale.	
S	Monitor of circuits to track compromises; lead to self-compliance/report.	

(*Continued*)

Table 4.1 (*Continued*)   Factors That Relate to Vulnerability and Consequence

CATEGORY	CORE CATEGORY = C, OR SUB-CATEGORY = S	CONTROL (COUNTER/ MITIGATION)
S	Develop and implement portal technology.	
S	Tag and meta-tag.	
S	Recognize importance of information security.	
S	Set up dummy accounts when needed (external who need access).	
S	Understanding generational differences in technology experience (risks at every age group that may be different).	
S	Use secure tethering applications.	
S	Use bit lockers for laptops.	
S	Use random and nonrandom screening with sensor technology.	
S	Imaging or reimaging.	
S	Proof of training so ignorance can't be pleaded.	
S	Peers and management should have oversight.	
S	Mitigate by making consequences known.	
C	**E. Organizational Resilience**	
S	Increase awareness.	
S	Increase competency of information security hygiene.	
S	Apply mitigation measures.	
S	Identify vulnerabilities and consequences of those vulnerabilities.	
S	Incorporate storytelling to create cyber-analog bilingualism.	
S	Link IT security performance to evaluations and bonuses.	

All insider threat factors, including unintended insider threat factors, are related in some way to risk, vulnerability, and consequence. This is important to understand. Everything that I have discussed in the prior chapter including human behavioral risk factors as typologies, organizational process risk factors, physical environmental risk factors, architectural IT system wellness risk factors, aggravated risk mitigation approach, and unknown factors, all relate. Additional vulnerabilities are listed under Core Category A as sub-categories. Consequences can vary on multiple levels as indicated on Core Category B and can be imposed as a form of punishment by an organization to an employee. However, consequences are typically viewed as part of a larger net cast with a cascade of delayed organizational consequences coming later, rather than just the consequence of individual accountability. As indicated in Core Category C and D, there are problems related to the discovery of consequences as related to specific actions, as well as a delay in assessing immediate mitigation measures because of the problems related to discovery of consequences.

Through continued research and investigation, as well as examining best practices and lessons learned, such as those factors identified in the tables of this book, organizational assessments can be improved, along with the creation of a course of action for risk mitigation.

Primary examples of factors that relate to vulnerability and consequence are presented as follows:

- All factors of insider threat relate to vulnerability and consequence
- Consequences are complex and have different levels of impact
- Problematic linkages with process and consequences
- Mitigation considerations
- Resilience factors

Additionally, a theme emerged that should also be considered is the need for cyber-physical digital-analog bilingualism. This term emerged from my initial study and is defined, as a need for not just translation and to linearly interpret risk from one area and explain it into another, but to be able to holistically understand the dynamics of both worlds, at the same time, in both languages, not just interpretation but bilingual.

Imagine the potential organizational enhancement with a greater depth of understanding of risk from both the physical and virtual dimensions. Humans live and operate in both the physical and virtual worlds, and there is a greater need to better understand them together. Within the organization, a need exists for a better understanding of the interconnected dimensions of today's employees who transcend between both the physical-virtual worlds that could open up a whole new approach to success.

4.2 All Factors of Insider Threat and How They Relate to Vulnerability and Consequence

All insider threat factors, including unintended insider threat factors are related in some way to risk, vulnerability, and consequence. Traditional security including physical security and cyber information technology security are interrelated. Essentially, every threat factor identified can be mapped to a vulnerability, or consequence. The degree of threat, or threat level and associated risk may be unknown, but it can be calculated or estimated based on an organizational assessment.

What is deemed as an acceptable level of risk to an organization, as well as what is not acceptable, needs to be understood and known, Understanding what the acceptable level of risk is, and having someone like the chief operating officer and the chief information officer actually accept this risk with eyes wide-open—the right someone who has the authority to do so within an organization—has become increasingly important. Understanding what they are accepting is also important. This acceptance might transcend into a certain number of settled cases, or losses, written off as the cost of doing business. However, remember that with technology the consequence may not be realized until well into the future.

If a business relies on a particular technology to transport all of its goods to a distributor and that technology is compromised by an insider threat, depending on the perishability of the product beyond shipping delays, the product could be destroyed. Whereas a large company could likely absorb the financial impact, a smaller company might not be able to absorb the financial loss. Having both data backups as well as critical system backups is important. From the physical domain, there is still risk to technology in the form of fires, floods, tornados, earthquakes, and other natural hazards, as well as man-made violent acts such as workplace violence including criminal or acts of terror.

Vulnerabilities are created by all employees, regardless of whether vulnerabilities are recognized or not by the employee or by a monitoring system. Insider threat risk factors including human behavioral risk factors as typologies; organizational process risk factors; physical environmental risk factors; architectural IT system wellness risk factors;

aggravated risk mitigation approaches; and unknown factors, all contribute and are part of the risk landscape that was discussed earlier in
the book. You may have an opportunity to narrow the frequency and
occurrences of various scenarios from occurring within your organization. An important concept to remember is that the threat is inside,
but the threat is also waiting outside the organization, for just that
right entry. The threat inside the organization creates the vulnerability
that can be exploited by many sources just waiting or searching for
that opening.

However, it is not just the people that create the vulnerabilities
mentioned. Technologically every system, network, and software
program will have a number of vulnerabilities. Technological maintenance is imperative to a healthy IT system. Organizations must
ensure that current software versions are on the network and that old
or outdated versions are effectively removed, and that regular scans
are on a cycle and vulnerabilities isolated and patched when found.
As discussed in the prior chapter, ensuring what doesn't need to be
on the network is actually removed from the network. Purchase of a
software program probably should not be treated as a single purchase,
unless it happens to be for a one-off short-term project—and even
then, it should not be installed on the main network but rather on a
stand-alone. Instead a software program purchase should be viewed
in light of a longer-term IT life cycle. Over the course of a decade, if
particular software is used, the amount of times new licensing or certificates have to be purchased could be rather expensive. Holding on
to older software versions could create substantive risk. Recalling this
software will be important, as the security perimeter is only as good as
the most updated software that is operating on your systems. Laptops
that are potentially out of date should not be plugged into a computer network; rather, dated laptops should be turned over to an IT
department to assess the viability of the laptop. Many organizations
have stand-alone computers. These stand-alone computers are typically subject to being overlooked and run the risk of not getting the
proper updates on a routine and timely basis. It is important to assume
the worst with technology—has it been patched? Probably not unless
it has been verified. The standard user typically does not have enough
background to understand if they have the most updated proper software version to meet or exceed minimum security specifications.

Organizations must also ensure that third-party contractors return all proprietary hardware, software, and intellectual property. Once contractors are no longer working on a contract, or employees are no longer employed on a particular work project, documents should be returned and all access privileges revoked. An out-of-date user privilege list creates a huge vulnerability. A process should be built into the acquisitions cycle. An organization needs to know what is/was actually shared—hardware, software, protected intellectual data—and should know at all times what actually needs to be returned and/or deleted. Should a breach occur, or information be spilled by a former employee or contractor, there should be accountability measures in place. Contracts and employee non-disclosure process and forms should be provided up-front and not after the fact. Initially, from known factors, vulnerabilities can be examined in contract language. The same technological, or higher level of scrutiny, should be required. Simple user names and passwords in the workplace are typically not adequate without a secondary factor of authentication. Passwords can be easily shared. When an organization is dealing with contracts and third-party vendors, it is really difficult to manage, without strict guidelines, who has access to the networks and computers that a company's product is being worked on. Subcontracting becomes even riskier, depending on the nature of the product.

4.3 Consequences Are Complex and Have Different Levels of Impact

Seemingly, organizations are being hijacked for their proprietary information, but they don't realize it until after the scheme has run its course and millions of dollars are potentially lost. In the virtual world, because of the digital revolution, almost every business record exists in digital form. This is the new business risk landscape. Whereas new technologies make it easier to conduct business, it also significantly increases the likelihood of instant loss of intellectual capital, including trade secrets especially those without vigilant monitoring in place.

During President Obama's last term, the United States issued the *Administration Strategy on Mitigating the Theft of U.S. Trade Secrets* from the White House. The administration clearly recognized the great loss of U.S. trade secrets and challenges in the ever-changing risk landscape. The strategy included contributions from the "Departments of

Commerce, Defense, Homeland Security, Justice, State, Treasury, the Office of the Director of National Intelligence and the Office of the United States Trade Representative," and was reflective of the "research and reporting of the Department of Commerce and Defense as well as the Office of the National Counterintelligence Executive."[1] This strategy highlights the need to counter intellectual theft, as well as the various federal offices that have significant equity in the process. The role of the U.S. Department of Commerce is often forgotten, even in prior election years with uninformed congressional/presidential candidates calling for the elimination of this department, which by the way also manages U.S. Census data.

Unlike other intellectual property protection, when a trade secret becomes publicly disclosed, there is no longer a property right. That protection will only remain a trade secret when the owner has taken steps to protect and maintain the secrecy—essentially a *continual vigilance* is required. In the world of information technology, this of course is a risk. Once an electronic document has been leaked and gone viral on the internet, retrieval and/or removal from the web is nearly impossible and incredibly difficult at best due to the repeatability of servers and social media sharing throughout the world. Unfortunately, once a trade secret is leaked or posted to a website, the trade secret will now be *generally known* and will very quickly lose trade secret status.

In early 2012, Sergey Aleynikov was released from prison after serving nearly a year for the theft of intellectual property. Mr. Aleynikov, a computer programmer at Goldman Sachs, was convicted of stealing computer code that had cost over $500 million to develop. Upon resigning from Goldman Sachs, he transferred proprietary information on his last day of work to his home computer. Despite investigation, conviction, and an initial sentencing to 97 months in federal prison, Mr. Aleynikov's conviction was overturned on appeal due to an interpretation and legal *loophole* of the U.S. Economic Espionage Act. This loophole was ultimately fixed with the Theft of Trade Secrets Clarification Act of 2012.[2] Theft of proprietary information will continue without significant consequence, as the reward is worth the risk in the eyes of the perpetrator.

However, even with several examples of theft in the literature, the penalties are comparatively moderate due to the potential monetary gain that the insider might experience even if caught. Ultimately, the security protection and prevention of leakage remains the responsibility of the owner of the information. Voluntary recommendations from the administration to organizations and companies included review of their "internal operations and policies to determine if current approaches are mitigating the risks and factors associated with trade secret misappropriation competed by both corporate and state sponsors," and that some of these areas could include *research and development compartmentalization, information security policies, physical security policies* as well as *human resource policies*.[3] With much greater detail, the tables and context within this book directly address insider threat: assessment and mitigation of risks in a holistic way, well beyond the headers of the administration's recommendations.

Research and development is an area of risk from a proprietary standpoint with regard to loss, but also from a system risk if not conducted outside the primary network. Having an internal facing network that does not reach the outside internet is certainly one mitigating measure, as well as applying many of the best practices of security for both cybersecurity as well as traditional security to safeguard materials. Ensuring connections or openness cannot be established within the research and development community is another way to mitigate this risk. This, however, must be monitored. Assuming a system is a closed system is simply not enough. Competitors may be consistently seeking top talent from competing organizations. Guarding against this kind of personnel loss is a priority for organizations, yet losses continue to happen as highly skilled personnel are highly mobile. Investigating the illusions of security will be important for organizations to make gains in protecting themselves. A robust cadre of organizational leadership should include interdisciplinary teams comprised of systems engineers with computer technology security experience and human resources personnel with traditional and cybersecurity experience, to elevate an organizations security profile to an entirely new level. Organizations should be highly proactive and buy the best talent and security they can afford, to best mitigate this risk and ultimately stack the deck in their favor. The potential consequences of inadequate security protocols include monetary consideration or payoff, loss of proprietary data, data breaches, damage to reputation, the embedded Trojan horse, and the list goes on. As a recap, an aggressive and robust management team is needed to address human behavioral risk factors as typologies; organizational process risk factors; physical environmental risk factors; architectural IT system wellness risk factors; aggravated risk mitigation approach and unknown factors; as well as the core categories identified in this chapter.

4.4 Problematic Linkages with Processes and Consequences

There are problematic linkages with process and consequence. Setting aside the network vulnerabilities and system catastrophic consequences for a moment, I will examine the federal punishment deterrents that are in place to prevent intentional economic crimes of the vengeful and malicious insider. In 2002, it was assessed by the U.S. Sentencing Commission that white-collar criminals were convicted and sentenced at much lower confinement levels than blue-collar crimes, which included theft and property destruction at the same financial levels. Essentially, the penalties tables at the federal level for economic crimes were not particularly high, were not equivalent to blue-collar crimes, nor were they seemingly based on a criminal deterrence construct.

However, after 2002 sentencing accountability for white-collar crimes were enhanced as a result of the Sarbanes-Oxley Act of 2002[4] (which focused on corporate accountability in the wake of recent white-collar crime such as Enron[5]). As a result of Sarbanes-Oxley, the U.S. Sentencing Commission[6] conducted follow-on action stemming from U.S. congressional direction to toughen sentences and reduce probation opportunities for fraud, embezzlement, and other economic crimes, such as fraud against the elderly, computer crimes, identity theft, and cellular cloning. The impact of these changes more than doubled the sentences for corporate officer fraud offenses and obstruction of justice offenses.[7]

However, despite this best effort, federal mandatory sentences were later appealed in the *United States vs. Booker*[8] case. As a result, the sentencing tables became *effectively advisory* and any enhanced sentence given by a judge (other than a prior conviction) that was not found by a jury or admitted by a defendant was a violation of the Sixth Amendment,[9] a U.S. constitutional right given to those under criminal prosecution. I would assert that the impact of white-collar crime on individuals needs even more research, and a greater understanding about the cascading consequences, as well as delayed impact of consequences to an organization as well as an individual. As increased traceability with insider threat occurs, I would expect that increased sentences could be then defended, and causality established beyond a reasonable doubt.

Daniel Richman summarizes that white-collar crime is different than other violent crimes with regard to deterrence. For example, unlike gun crime deterrence, the government does not gather the executives of white-collar crime to learn from sentences given to peers.[10] The priorities of violent crime, due to political pressure of enforcement, has perhaps given way to the opportunity cost of white-collar crime enforcement and related deterrence.

Although the awareness of white-collar crime has increased, including with vengeful and malicious insider threat, the prevalence of more frequent prosecution has not necessarily occurred except in more extreme public media circumstances, such as was the media frenzy surrounding the collapse of Enron. Enron was once considered to be an innovative e-commerce company grounded with the perceived stability of traditional utility companies. Enron created a world of futures including utility futures, lobbying Congress for deregulation in gas and electric producers, thereby creating a market for trading futures in gas and electric power utilities.[11] Instead of stability, this company was on shaky ground, significantly overstating its performance and deliberately hiding its debts and heavy losses in its partnership acquisitions. Executives had already pocketed millions and significantly donated to the campaigns of both House and Senate Republican and Democratic parties. Enron's auditability became difficult after orders for document shredding was given by the company's lead auditor. The company imploded and billions were lost to investors and employees. The former CEO of Enron, Jeffery Skillings, was sentenced to 24 years in prison resulting from 19 counts of conspiracy, securities fraud, and insider trading, and lying to auditors. His sentence was later reduced to 14 years in 2013, ending years of ongoing appeals in a deal agreement.[12] Whereas $40 million of his assets had been frozen, these funds would be distributed to victims; additionally, a challenged error in sentencing would be factored into this reduced sentence.

However, regarding these white-collar crimes, which ultimately stole the life savings of thousands of people, the question that should be asked is: Do these penalties justify as an effective deterrent? With this example, greed was a culprit, an unsustainable effort that did not follow proper accounting practices. Enron was a big company, but ultimately not a sustainable one in the market. Decisions by investors were made with deceptive fraudulent information by the most senior in the organization. The cascading consequences of such a loss could potentially be argued that poor heath or even death could have befallen those who had been employed, having lost their healthcare and their life savings. However, the scope of consequences within a white-collar crime does not typically factor this in for sentencing, instead linking to the number of people impacted and dollar values.

Now, let's shift back to vulnerabilities and consequences within a network. Sometimes a wicked employee as an insider threat might know the cause of an error because they were the one who created the error. However, this insider may feel that self-reporting would be detrimental to their future and not report the error or perhaps defer blame to something else. For example, if a technician runs a test that creates a problem in the network, and the test was not an approved operation resulting in a significant loss of data and/or access to the network for part of the company, the technician is likely to not want to disclose this error.

Many issues can potentially be traced, but deniability takes place even internally. Losing one's job could be a realistic deterrent for reporting errors caused by oneself. Ensuring that several people are responsible for this testing, and that there is an accountability chain can minimize such an occurrence from happening. Additionally, having highly skilled personnel to immediately research and investigate is critical, along with 24/7 monitoring and response.

Sometimes the privileged user will make a catastrophic error following all the proper processes, but at other times, they may not have followed a proper process, or that process may not be properly documented. Remember that information technology experts are quite good at navigating through systems with much higher level permissions within various systems. Organizations are typically good at rewarding out of the box thinking, but sometimes the behavior of experts will fall soundly into the virtuous or wicked categories.

In contrast, it is not common to see an organization incentivize the disclosure of errors by its employees, or disclosure of errors by colleagues, which unfortunately often has to happen. Oftentimes the fingerprint on these errors are traceable, while at other times can be quite difficult. As the saying goes, no one likes a rat, a tattletale, a squealer, but organizations need this process. Even as I write this it seems counter to loyalty and team building. A distinction where loyalty to person and loyalty to organization must be developed. Clearly, this is much easier said than done. For this reason, there are some whistleblower protection laws on the books for federal employees.

For a short duration in 2016, the U.S. Department of Defense incentivized testing and reporting for their public facing websites and systems where registered participants could receive a payout if they discovered vulnerabilities. Research from this pilot was rolled forward with partners from the Software Engineering Institute (SEI) of Carnegie Mellon University with the Department of Defense Cyber Crime Center (DC3) to set up a Department of Defense Vulnerability Disclosure Program (DVDP).[13] Whereas this program is specific to the Department of Defense, there are a number of best practices provided open source because of their sponsored research.[14] This research should be reviewed by organizations and businesses on how to adapt or align best practices to manage the vulnerabilities contained within software and software-based products. There are some very good examples on how to organize and coordinate, and although there is probably not one right answer for every business or organization, there is now significantly more literature available to assist with internal assessment and mitigation of risk.

One of the problematic linkages with process is that within a business or organization, the processes are absent and/or they are not set up properly in order to discover or identify vulnerabilities, report them, and properly fix them through patches or configurations. There are many different types of software and products that use software, as well as different types of vendors that may or may not be immediately able to respond to provide fixes for the identified vulnerabilities. Whereas some fixes may be more easily adapted, such as software as a service through application for which these patches can be deployed more quickly. In networked systems, sometimes there is a central hub that will need to take the patches and redistribute the patches to the affected terminals. If the configuration of that hub is off or the infrastructure is not adequate, then the patches may not deploy. Not all fixes can be distributed remotely as there may be physical replacement of infrastructure that has to occur. This replacement can be costly in terms of both dollars and time. A lot of scanning and testing can be done upon networks; however, all reports should not be fully trusted either. Reports can be forced to falsify reality by an insider or the technology used to create the reports could have become compromised itself. In dealing with the testing environment, an isolated testing environment would be more ideal before launching, because it can be risky to develop a response and manage vulnerability remediation on the same software or system that is already compromised.

I was directly involved in a U.S. Coast Guard cybersecurity surge response in late summer of 2015, shortly after the release of the U.S. Coast Guard Cyber Strategy in June, which outlined three strategic objectives: defending cyberspace, enabling operations, and protecting infrastructure.[15] This Coast Guard strategy had been in development since late in 2013 and approved after convincing senior leadership of the importance of such focused efforts; as it was being written a huge organizational cultural shift occurred, and conceptually cyberspace as an operational domain was fully embraced.

The Coast Guard's cybersecurity surge response was named the Cyber Crisis Action Team Delta (Cyber CAT Δ), in part because of the primary strategic objective of defending cyberspace, and the Δ representing the change. Cyber CAT Δ was a groundbreaking incident command system response that brought together both operational and technical experts to respond to critical cybersecurity challenges for the Coast Guard, and in response to the presidential mandate to increase cybersecurity across the federal government. Fast forward to 2018; this innovative response, using a traditional all-hazards physical response structure has concluded and been reported in open source articles and discussed in panels by then forward thinking chief information security officer Glenn Hernandez and chief information officer and commander of Coast Guard Cyber Command Marshall Lytle, III. My experience is a direct one, the response was developed in collaboration with Coast Guard Cyber Command, the chief information security officer, along with surge response experts and the blessing of the chief information officer,

the deputy commandant for mission support, the deputy commandant for operations, the vice commandant, and the commandant.
My story is kept at a strategic level, narrowed in scope to the topic,
and contains only what could be considered open source information
that has already been released openly.

During our development of the concept of operations for Cyber
CAT Δ, we quickly realized that quite a lot of our computer infrastructure had been categorized like a fixed asset, such as a piece of
furniture or wall art rather than an ongoing information technology investment that needed more frequent maintenance and ongoing
reinvestment in its infrastructure. We quickly assessed that to operate
and maintain functional capabilities, there were significant gaps to
address. There were no instructions on how to standardize or fix configuration uniformly across the organization enterprise, and therefore
a lot of virtuous and wicked insiders had made several configuration
changes in order to keep the network running on a backbone of erod-
ing infrastructure. Yes, some of the network was secure, but certainly
not all. We were unable to measure just how secure with a high level
of confidence, because we could not see our network fully at the time.

What was operating in the shorter term allowing software and systems to function in order to accomplish a mission was a threat, and a
significantly increased cybersecurity risk to the network in the longer
term, and with very little regard to continuing maintenance in a standardized way. The Coast Guard is really good at rescue, and our cybersecurity posture was in extremus. In an era of the OPM breaches, this
was less than ideal. What was missing was indeed a uniformly known
standard and repair process similar to maintenance procedure cards,
as well as infrastructure reinvestment, accountability, and awareness
that information technology is everyone's concern, not just those who
keep the system up and running. Sure the chief information officer
was smart, and the team of information technology specialists talented, but that was perhaps a potential downfall and counter to standard configuration management. Making it work, saving the day, is
what specialists were all about. This however, is much different than
ensuring organizational cybersecurity and being able to detect the
insider threat. If alarms were going off everywhere, how could the
real threat be assessed properly, and then isolated? It was a challenge.
In my estimation, there was (in part) an illusion of cybersecurity and

the organizational infrastructure and standard configuration needed expeditious virtual and physical discovery and remediation.

One of the problems we assessed in Cyber CAT Δ had been attributed to a perceived lack of bandwidth; this lack of bandwidth was thought to be responsible for not properly getting updates to the enterprise software and systems, many of these core-to-business function and operational mission performance. If only more bandwidth could be purchased, surely this would solve all the delays of remediation. However, as we quickly found out, there was another culprit responsible for the increased risk. It was soon discovered that several of the computer hubs had been improperly configured, and therefore were not capable of redistribution of the patches to the many computers within the network. Basically, there was a continual feedback loop of trying to load the patches, creating a constant busy signal. The causality was not bandwidth, instead patching was in a state of perpetual delay as a consequence primarily because of not having standard configurations. Not even just standard configurations of what was known, but a lot of what was not known but residing on the network in areas that had not been properly mapped. Both lack of infrastructure, and nonstandard configurations were blocking the distribution of very necessary and very critical updates. The corrections would require a combined approach of planners, network computer engineers, as well as physical security specialists and operators to discover a pathway and way forward to full security compliance. This cybersecurity problem quickly required a serious boots-on-the-ground approach.

A much higher level of competency was required, and interdisciplinary subject matter experts had to be called in. A process had to be negotiated and determined, and while this process was evolving, it also had to be adaptable and agile. As new discoveries were made, new challenges would arise, and they had to be addressed as part of the overall concept of operations. Along with this diverse group of experts, senior executives needed to be educated and budgets redistributed. Ownership and accountability at the most senior level had to be established and made traceable. Who owned the systems, who was responsible for the systems at the executive level, and did they know it? This sounds simple, but in some organizations systems may be owned across a number of diverse entities, and security investment may be disparate. Getting interdisciplinary owners together to rally around a common and expensive cause, can be difficult, but is critical to success. System owners must understand what their cascading consequences of being unsecure could lead to. In some cases, these systems might simply have to be shut down if they are too risky. For operations, having a critical system be stopped could be a big enough warning to shore up the system effectively, even if it was a costly investment. In the shorter term, it keeps the business secure and operational to actually conduct business.

Because of aging infrastructure, the remote quick-fix repair that had been planned and thought to be more readily available took several more months to fully discover and identify more of the vulnerabilities and to remediate, meaning fix and complete. Additionally, improving infrastructure required a significant financial investment, whereas a large organization might be able to shuffle around priorities, for any size organization, this can be difficult without having adequate resources and reserves, great loss can occur quickly. This type of unplanned investment might not be at the top of an organizations priority, especially if they do not have a traceable consequence. Before a breach occurs, without digital forensic investigation, these inadequacies are not always attributable to a particular consequence even when it is known that software and systems that use software products are not in optimal working order.

Ensuring that a network is fully mapped, that what is supposed to be on it, is, and what is not supposed to be on it, isn't, may easily require a discovery and remediation ground team in conjunction with a cybersecurity team to run scans to help to focus on high risk areas, and quickly remediate. To summarize, in order to complete the Cyber CAT Δ, the process that was used to facilitate this action was an the incident command system with a response layered on a cybersecurity problem. It was certainly a trial of process, and an innovative effort to gain a focused attention on a problem in an era of post-OPM data breach and the subsequent 2015 federal Cybersecurity Sprint response.[16] For the time it did work, efforts were focused and it led to significant organizational change as a spin off from the incident response, reimagining logistics, IT investment, program management oversight, cybersecurity oversight, and data analytics.

Leadership played an important role, and the incident command system general staff and incident commander were critical to success.

Additionally, we all came to love the operation section chief James "Jim" Cash's expertise, drive, and humor. He served as an inspirational leader who set the course, aligned resources, and was motivational in order to achieve cybersecurity discipline across four major lines of effort including strong authentication, device hardening, reducing the attack surface, and alignment to cybersecurity/computer network defense service providers.[17]

Response can be complicated, and in that same lens, there is another problem process related to consequences surrounding vender vulnerability response capability. While consumers of software products, business and organizations should not be alone in creating solutions; instead, vendors should have a lead role. But there are a lot of challenges in vendor products related to security to consider. Internet of Things (IOT) products may have been developed with inadequate threat models that underestimate the realities of a hostile threat landscape.

The SEI is described as having awareness that vendors of software-centric products are less than optimal because several vendors lacked an ability within their product life cycle to identify vulnerability, and even had difficulty accepting identified vulnerabilities. SEI assesses that this weakness is in part because some vendors are small and may not have adequately developed a security incidence response capability for their product[18] and/or the vendor lacks internet security capability despite being highly competent in their specific engineering area of expertise. Essentially, a lack of quality assurance practice because the impact of the IOT has not been factored in and the vendor has not adequately considered the network in which the product is reliant upon and which is enabling the product.[19]

As part of an acquisition cycle for software, the entire life cycle of security needs to be factored in. This includes the ability to identify vulnerabilities, relay them, or receive notice of them from the vendor, and having the ability to remediate. Also in some cases, a business might be placed in the position that a fix will never be available and then additional decision-making needs to occur in order to mitigate the risk. A risk mitigation strategy might be that particular software is recalled within the organization and investment is made into more secure software that can produce the same result. Or shifting to more cloud-based application-based software when the option is a viable one.

The increase of cloud-accessible applications over the next decade is expected to increase significantly; however, our reliance overall on software-based products will only continue to increase, as our behavioral demands ask for more and more convenience and reliance and the threat landscape continues to rise, as does our dependency and potential consequences lurking in our future.

4.5 Mitigation Considerations

In contrast, as organizations gain a better understanding of insider threat including the organizational risks presented in Chapter 3, they can get a better grasp on how to shore up their risk and gain improved control surrounding their potential circumstances. One of the areas I've continued to stress throughout my career related to cybersecurity is the need for 24/7 monitoring and response, as has already been discussed. Both human and computer monitoring and testing are necessary.

An organization needs an astute chief information officer as well as an innovative chief information security officer that works in tandem with traditional security roles. These positions greatly contribute to an organization's higher-level goals, reputation preservation, business loss prevention, liability reduction, and bankruptcy avoidance. With increased monitoring, network oversight, accountability, and advanced prestaged responders for incidents that do occur, vulnerability as well as consequence can be greatly reduced. A focus on mitigation considerations and actions for resilience are also described in this chapter.

Not only are costly compromises in the United States repeatedly occurring, and frequently of personal data, but U.S. companies and the U.S. government are typically late to identify that the breach has occurred and/or are late to inform their customers of the breach. Unlike some other nations within the European Union, the U.S. expectations of privacy are actually quite limited. I would assert that U.S. laws have not protected their citizens well enough and that more accountability and legal regulation is needed, in this era, to better protect its citizens against insider threats, increasing cybersecurity breaches and their potential, not just actual consequences. Right now, simply having a breach does not typically create a liability, individuals must prove how they have been harmed by such a breach; traceability to a particular compromise can be difficult to prove by the average citizen. With continued media frenzied privacy compromises like Equifax, Yahoo!, and Facebook, the U.S. Congress is taking note. On the other hand, the U.S. government has been one of the biggest offenders, so in part there is a conflict.

In contrast with the United States, privacy laws are more restrictive in the European Union. A new law in the European Union that was issued through a European Commission Regulation, changes the way telecommunications companies are required to notify authorities and individuals of personal data breaches, which includes additional prevention measures against social harm, physical harm, significant humiliation or damage of reputation, should a breach not be adequately or swiftly addressed.[20] The penalty for not complying tops 1,000,000 euros or 2 percent of an organization's global annual revenue. This European Union law acknowledges the extended harm to individuals, or organizations; however, it is limited to telecommunications companies whereas these are not the only entities that will likely have data breaches that compromise privacy. Perhaps the limited scope of the regulation was intended to protect the governments who are also holders of a significant amount of personal data. Even if accountability liability laws have not yet caught up with demand, more information is needed about vulnerabilities and consequences. Maintaining a positive reputation is one of the greatest concerns of a large corporation, especially where there is significant competition.

4.6 Organizational Resilience Factors

Organizational resilience is part of what this question is focused upon. Increasing awareness, competency of information security hygiene, identifying vulnerabilities and consequences, the application of mitigation measures, along with incorporating storytelling to further cyber-physical digital-analog bilingualism, and linking information technology security performance to evaluations and bonuses was identified.

Awareness can be increased through a number of organizational avenues, depending on the nature of the organization. Strategic communications should be assessed. Not every communication will be sent the same way with the same messaging, but linking awareness of insider threat, as applied to all employees with all employees being accountable is a start. Educating how to best reduce risk by practicing improved information security hygiene, the previous chapter tables offer excellent starting points. The insider threat is not just a chief information officer problem; it expands across every organization and business and impacts all aspects of operation including the profitability or the ability to deliver mission readiness and mission performance. Human behavior must be proactively managed as part of a mitigation measure. Ethical values should ideally align with an organization's purpose. If it does not, there will be even more increased risk. Organizational assessments are useful in helping to understand workplace culture. Cultural shifts must occur in order for organizations to become more proactive in security, with both traditional and cybersecurity being important. Every employee, every person who has a connection to the organization, has an important role. Incentivizing the reporting of possible security vulnerabilities is one such mitigation measure that could be put in place. Stories must be told, stories to reinforce the positives, the negatives, the accountabilities, and the lessons learned. In proprietary competition, as I understand it, the sharing of stories can also be considered a threat. Creating meaningful stories without increasing risk will continue to be important. Stories can be told without giving away proprietary information, or showcasing the weakness in an organization. Storytelling can be delayed also, so that once the vulnerability has been fixed, the story can be shared as a best practice.

An organization that provides very good insight, at a strategic level, into the latest larger scams in a readable and meaningful way, in what I would consider storytelling, happens to be the American Association of Retired Persons (AARP).[21] A quick search inside their fraud watch network portal highlights the lessons learned from consequences already experienced as well as potential impacts to an individual. Many of the frauds and scams summarized by AARP, as you would guess, are targeted at older adults who in many cases have life savings of various amounts that make swindling lucrative. Although this organization's mission is scoped to those over age 50, I highly recommend their resources to any adult. AARP provides push alert notifications and an avenue for members to report fraud and obtain peer counseling, support, and referrals for additional reporting and assistance.

In 2017, the DHS streamlined several organizational structures, moving US-CERT, ICS-CERT, and the NCC (Information Sharing and Analysis Center for Telecommunications) into a central hub for cyber-threat sharing between government and the private sector. Now called the National Cybersecurity and Communications Integration Center (NCCIC),[22] it is touted as the nation's flagship for cyber defense, incident response, and operational integration center. Their mission is to reduce the nation's risk of systemic cybersecurity and communications challenges. This resource has an outward-facing presence for engagement with industry and it contains several resources including bulletins on weekly vulnerability summaries that are recorded by the NIST and the National Vulnerabilities Database, which is sponsored by DHS and the NCCIC/US-CERT. I would recommend that any organization have an ongoing connection with this entity, in order to be able to address vulnerabilities, before they are exploited. Additionally, there is an avenue for users to securely report incidents, report indicators, report phishing, and submit malware artifacts. Stories can be obtained through many sources, the NCCIC is one avenue.

4.7 Practical Mental Models Continued

I micro-analyzed the triangular aspects shared among cyber, physical, and humans, along with all the interconnected core categories. I felt that development of the cyber-physical digital-analog bilingualism concept was necessary to specifically highlight the need for a better understanding of the interconnected dimensions of today's employees that transcend between both physical-virtual worlds; to not just linearly interpret risk from one area and explain it in another, but to be able to holistically understand the dynamics of both worlds, at the same time, in both languages; interpretation and bilingual.

4.7.1 Mental Model (Aspect 5) Cyber-Physical Digital-Analog Bilingualism

Aspect 5 is *a grounded theory aspect of the need for cyber-physical digital-analog bilingualism.* The theory of cyber-physical digital-analog bilingualism was developed, and this new term emerged in my micro-analysis to describe the need for humans who live in both the physical and virtual worlds and to better understand both worlds that they frequent.

This theoretical conceptualization may help organizations to prioritize the development of their managers, or employees at large. Those who are bilingual should be able to share their knowledge with those who are less familiar with the concepts, and to assist with the risk mitigation process, and determine what acceptable risk is, and what is not. This understanding may also help to drive organizations to enhance their core competency requirements for information technology security at large. I have created the interconnected figure to depict the cyber-physical digital-analog bilingualism competency (see Figure 4.1).

As stated at the beginning of this chapter:

All insider threat factors, including unintended insider threat factors, are related to risk, vulnerability, and consequence. Physical security is very much interconnected to information technology security, and cyber-physical digital-analog bilingualism is called for. Organizational resilience is connected to understanding factors related to vulnerability and their consequences, along with process related to consequences and risk mitigation measures. Linking awareness, increasing competency, applying mitigation measures, storytelling, and linking performance to evaluations and rewards may enhance organizational resilience.

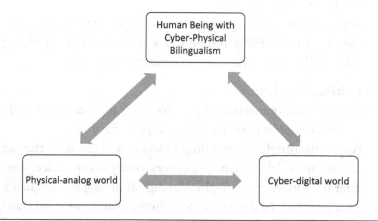

Figure 4.1   Cyber-physical digital-analog bilingualism.

If vulnerabilities are understood, organizations may be able to effectively reduce these vulnerabilities by applying a proactive approach, or plan for occurrences should they manifest. Having a process is especially important. Consequences, however, can be fundamentally difficult to connect to some actual occurrences, although not all. The next chapters in the book describe the roles and approaches that are taken by managers and information technology specialists to mitigate organizational risk.

Appendix: Best Practice—Practical Knowledge and Practitioner Application

Practical knowledge
- Know that vulnerability is the insider threat factor that allows for exploitation or susceptibility, creating an event, incident, or occurrence of traditional and cybersecurity; the consequence is the result of the exploitation or susceptibility.
- Understand that consequences may be delayed with information technology, and that the cause and effect relationship is not overt.
- Recognize that the virtuous, wicked, vengeful, and malicious insider threats create vulnerabilities, where cascading consequences may be felt on multiple levels extending outside the organization its direct external partners.
- Learn that all factors of insider threat are related to vulnerability and consequence.
- Recognize response options available to you in your particular industry to effectively respond to a crisis situation involving vulnerability and minimize potential consequence.

Practitioner application
- Ensure that organizational process exists to discover/identify vulnerabilities, report them and properly fix them.
- Apply meaningful storytelling practice, and consider the use of mental models to reinforce cybersecurity best practice; consider the model of cyber-physical digital-analog bilingualism.
- Examine that the deterrence for white-collar crime is substantively less than violent crimes, and that additional protections

on trade secrets and other proprietary information must be enhanced to protect the insider threat.

- Prepare for the time when you have to respond to a larger-scale cybersecurity problem with a construct that is both culturally acceptable and flexible within your organization; develop a response plan.
- Ensure governance and process is in place for both the enforcement of, as well as reward for, security compliance.

Endnotes

1. Administration Strategy on Mitigating the Theft of U.S. Trade Secrets, Executive Office of the President of the United States. February 2013. Retrieved from https://www.justice.gov/criminal-ccips/file/938321/download.
2. Public Law 112-236 The Theft of Trade Secrets Clarification Act of 2112 (S. 3642). December 28, 2012.
3. Administration Strategy on Mitigating the Theft of U.S. Trade Secrets, Executive Office of the President of the United States. February 2013. Retrieved from https://www.justice.gov/criminal-ccips/file/938321/download.
4. Sarbanes-Oxley Act of 2002 [Public Law 107-204]. Retrieved from https://www.congress.gov/107/plaws/publ204/PLAW-107publ204.pdf.
5. The Fall of Enron. NPR. 2002. Retrieved from https://www.npr.org/news/specials/enron/.
6. United States Sentencing Commission. Retrieved from https://www.ussc.gov/.
7. The Sentencing Commission's Implementation of the Sarbanes-Oxley Act by John R. Steer, Member and Vice Chair of the U.S. Sentencing Commission, 2013. Retrieved from https://www.ussc.gov/sites/default/files/pdf/training/organizational-guidelines/selected-articles/Steer-PLI-2003.pdf.
8. 543 U.S. 220 (2005).
9. U.S. Bill of Rights, Amendment VI, December 15, 1791. Retrieved from https://www.archives.gov/founding-docs/bill-of-rights-transcript.
10. Federal White Collar Sentencing in the United States: A Work in Progress by Dan Richman. 2013. Retrieved from http://lcp.law.duke.edu.
11. The History of Enron. NPR 2002. Retrieved from https://www.npr.org/news/specials/enron/history.html.
12. Ex-Enron CEO Jeffrey Skilling's Prison Sentence Reduced to 14 Years. *Huffington Post*. June 21, 2013. Retrieved from https://www.huffingtonpost.com/2013/06/21/jeffrey-skilling-prison-sentence-reduced_n_3480145.html.

13. Researcher Art Manion. Reporting DoD Network Vulnerabilities Just Got Easier. Carnegie Mellon University. Software Engineering Institute: 2017 Year in Review.

14. The CERT Guide to Coordinated Vulnerability Disclosure. Software Engineering Institute: Carnegie Mellon University. Special Report CMU/SEI-2017-SR-022, Approved for Public Release, August 2017.

15. U.S. Coast Guard Cyber Strategy, June 2015.

16. The White House: President Barack Obama Archives (2015, July 31). Strengthening & Enhancing Federal Cybersecurity for the 21st Century. Retrieved from: https://obamawhitehouse.archives.gov/blog/2015/07/31/strengthening-enhancing-federal-cybersecurity-21st-century.

17. DoD Cybersecurity Discipline Implementation Plan (October 2015, as amended February 2016). Retrieved from https://dodcio.defense.gov/Portals/0/Documents/Cyber/CyberDis-ImpPlan.pdf.

18. The CERT® Guide to Coordinated Vulnerability Disclosure. Software Engineering Institute: Carnegie Mellon University. Special Report CMU/SEI-2017-SR-022, Approved for Public Release, August 2017.

19. Ibid.

20. EU Data Breach Notification Rule: The Key Elements by Laura Vivet Tana. April 16, 2018. Retrieved from https://iapp.org/news/a/eu-data-breach-notification-rule-the-key-elements/.

21. AARP website. https://www.aarp.org/.

22. NCCIC. About. www.us-cert.gov/.

5

MANAGERIAL AND INFORMATION TECHNOLOGY SPECIALIST APPROACHES TO MITIGATING RISK AND INCREASING ORGANIZATIONAL RESILIENCE

5.1 Introduction

In this chapter, I describe the roles and approaches of best practices taken by managers and information technology specialists to mitigate the organizational risk which is under their span of control, and organizational influence. Keep in mind that although distinct differences are captured here, there will be some similarity and some overlap because from organization to organization, variation in the scope of duties is likely to occur. For example, a manager may or may not be an information technology specialist, but may be in charge of a related program and have substantial influence in policy creation or decision making within an organization. Whereas an information technology specialist may also be a supervisor of other technologists, the specialist may not necessarily identify within the management role or leadership community of an organization. However, a specialist's advisory knowledge, if risen high enough in the hierarchy can make a substantive impact on the direction and governance of an organization. What I'm trying to articulate is that although there are some overlapping similarities between both the manager and the information technology specialist, there are also prevalent differences to their approaches, and this is worth knowing. Taking a deeper dive into this information can be beneficial to the assessment and mitigation of risk.

First, I provide a narrative response, as I did in the preceding chapter that directly answers how managers and information technology specialists mitigate risk to insider threat to organization, thereby enhancing organizational resilience. Toward the middle of the chapter, I enter into a more comprehensive discussion. Throughout the discussion, practical application, mental models, and best practices are called out. Specifically, the core categories and sub-categories may be used by an organization to identify if the particular functions are being applied within their organization and consider if the categories should be used within their respective organizations to mitigate risk. The tables are separated by the managerial approach, as well as the information technology specialist's approach, and in doing so I believe these distinctions are worth understanding from multiple vantage points within a given business or organization. A quick check accompanies these categorical findings to allow for a greater depth of review.

How do managers and information technology specialists mitigate risk to insider threat to organization, thereby enhancing organizational resilience? The answer is as follows.

5.1.1 *The Narrative Response*

- Both expert managers and information technology specialists contribute to the mitigation of risk to insider threat to organization, and thereby enhance organizational resilience in similar and different ways. Managers focus on application of management practice including actions related to developing business rules and guidelines and policing. Managers ideally ensure training and can share stories to help transcend and interpret cyber-physical reality, especially if their background is in information technology security. Information technology specialists follow rules and apply their subject matter expertise to monitor and detect. They focus on prevention, response, and their recovery related to incidents. They get the job done while developing their competency and provide advisement on issues to managers and employees. Training and knowledge are central to both the manager and the technology specialist. Asking the right question is an essential part of communications between the highly tasked manager and the information technology specialist.

- Communicating messages through a compelling chain of interpretation is needed to enhance decision making. Organizational resilience may be achieved through the managerial and the information technology categories that include training; applying textbook and practical management practice; developing business rules and guidelines and following them; telling stories that transcend cyber-physical reality; conducting managerial policing action; following rules for information security protection and prevention; applying subject matter expertise to monitor threats or detect compromise; preventing user error; responding to and recovering from incidents; developing self and applying critical thinking practice; getting the job done; and being an advisor to management.

5.1.2 The Categorical Response

I have just presented the narrative, so I will now list the categorical results. Although the role of the manger and the information technology specialist are intertwined and overlapping, there are distinct differences. These differences are displayed in Tables 5.1 and 5.2. These categorical results may be used in terms of an assessment to identify the organizational responsibility or lead and assigned control. Following both of the tables is a more descriptive discussion.

Both the manager and the information technology specialist play critical roles within an organization to ward against insider threat. They are your frontline insider threat defense and offense in the assessment and mitigation of risk. Executives not only need to ensure that talent is hired, but also continue to develop trust and allegiance with those who are hired.

This nurturing and allegiance development may not always be easy to develop due to the increase in transportability of information technology specialists between organizations. Competitive certifications may create lucrative opportunities for top talent to be recruited away from the organizations that they serve. However, many managers and specialists will have allegiance with their organizations, for reasons such as the mission or higher purpose of the organization, are more likely to stay. This allegiance should also be appreciated, and in turn recognized in a meaningful way.

Table 5.1 How *Managers* Mitigate Risk to Insider Threat to Organization, Thereby Enhancing Resilience

CATEGORY	CORE CATEGORY = C, OR SUB-CATEGORY = S	STATUS	
		CHECKOFF YES	CHECKOFF NO
C	**A. Training, Training, Training, Training**	**Checkoff Yes**	**Checkoff No**
S	Train everyone. Identify those who connect but are not being trained. Note network access, and timeliness of training.		
S	Emphasis of material sensitivity.		
S	Educate within the office.		
S	Ensure staff is aware of protocols within the network.		
S	Annual training.		
S	Refresher training—often.		
S	Organizational training.		
S	Change the way we train, look at new ways of delivery methods.		
S	Create new training—frequently due to threat changes.		
S	Train in person—this should not be left to online only.		
S	Ensure 100% training for future accountability if needed.		
S	More budget-minded training.		
S	In-house training.		
C	**B. Apply Good Textbook and Practical Management Practices**	**Checkoff Yes**	**Checkoff No**
S	Know what your people are going to do (though behavioral prediction is challenging).		
S	Continue monitoring of personnel, because life changes.		
S	Focus on "managing" even though as a manager there may not be much time because overtaxed with tasks.		
S	Be forward thinking.		
S	Ask techs for guidance on what you should be asking.		
S	Develop yourself and keep up-to-date on changing threats and technology.		
S	Ask for status reports, often.		
S	Recognize internal talent and seek technical interpretation to assist the management level.		
S	Pull in engineers and programs on front end of projects, not back end.		

(*Continued*)

Table 5.1 (*Continued*) How *Managers* Mitigate Risk to Insider Threat to Organization, Thereby Enhancing Resilience

CATEGORY	CORE CATEGORY = C, OR SUB-CATEGORY = S	STATUS	
		CHECKOFF YES	CHECKOFF NO
S	Hold all employees accountable for violations in security.		
S	Connect to the organizational structure for change and interactions; promote transparency, interoperability, and accountability.		
C	**C. Develop Business Rules and Guidelines, and Follow Them**	**Checkoff Yes**	**Checkoff No**
S	Manager needs to understand the need to identify IT security rules and what procedures are needed; create guidelines and then train and reinforce through training and spot-checks.		
S	Build in network safeguards to screen connections.		
S	Be solutions driven.		
S	Develop process, rules, policy to mitigate risk.		
S	Report cases as necessary to an established central security office.		
S	Apply and promote rule-based access.		
S	Ensure privileged users are qualified.		
S	Say no to unsafe storage, file share, or meeting place proposals.		
S	Say no to platforms where information security cannot be verified.		
S	Ensure common-access-card credentials are used.		
S	Push for the jump on implementing controls that are not used but could be.		
S	Follow pin-set rules.		
S	Use software to block specific internet sites.		
S	Forecast security controls to be used in the future.		
S	Have hands on participation.		
S	Review lessons learned; apply them.		
S	Ensure systemic safeguards.		
S	Redesign systems.		
S	Wear multiple hats (cyber and physical), and aim to be cyber-analog bilingual.		
S	Work with other subject matter experts.		

(Continued)

Table 5.1 (*Continued*)   How *Managers* Mitigate Risk to Insider Threat to Organization, Thereby Enhancing Resilience

CATEGORY	CORE CATEGORY = C, OR SUB-CATEGORY = S	STATUS	
		CHECKOFF YES	CHECKOFF NO
S	Look at business management models and practices for potential application.		
S	Organizational standards are needed for managers to hold employees to them.		
C	**D. Tell Stories That Transcend and Interpret the Cyber-Physical Realities**	**Checkoff Yes**	**Checkoff No**
S	Tell stories to subordinates that translate meaning and lead to comprehension and understanding of the individual.		
S	Tell stories to senior leadership that translate meaning and lead to comprehension and understanding.		
S	Articulate compelling stories that connect to the person receiving them. This can be difficult to do.		
S	Interpret cyber into analog context for understanding.		
S	Advocate for organizational stories to share with managers and crew.		
S	Investigate occurrences to develop new stories to prevent repeat offenses.		
S	Tell stories of the Intrusion Defense System.		
S	Tell stories of infected systems found on the network.		
S	Create monthly newsletter or notice to users. This could be used to shape positive computer uses, changes in behavior, etc.		
C	**E. Important Managerial Actions Related to Policing: Actions to Be Emphasized as Needed and/or Taken by a Program Manager**	**Checkoff Yes**	**Checkoff No**
S	Conduct random spot-checks, frequently.		
S	Ensure particular job task is managed with appropriate safeguards.		
S	Use electronic monitoring and screening systems.		
S	Have in-person monitoring.		
S	Apply electronic monitoring, within legal boundaries.		
S	Wear multiple hats, such as personnel, physical, and information systems. As all part of cybersecurity.		

(*Continued*)

Table 5.1 (*Continued*)   How *Managers* Mitigate Risk to Insider Threat to Organization, Thereby Enhancing Resilience

CATEGORY	CORE CATEGORY = C, OR SUB-CATEGORY = S	STATUS	
		CHECKOFF YES	CHECKOFF NO
s	Work with other subject matter experts.		
s	Determine accountability and conduct mini investigations with aim to prevent and reduce repeat offenses.		
s	Emphasize sensitivity of materials.		
s	Recognize their data's chain of custody from initial collection to final report.		
s	Recognize what everyone is trying to accomplish.		
s	Develop solutions to what is needed.		
s	Know the IT community inside.		
s	Know the IT community outside.		
s	Recognize different situations.		
s	Know top threats.		
s	Manage your alerts.		
s	Leverage technology to mitigate insider threat.		
s	Social aspects, leverage to help mitigate insider risk.		
s	Monitor of individuals work stages.		
s	Identify behavior of employees.		
s	Look for best interest of employee to prevent from doing something advert. This requires knowing more than the employee to prevent errors.		
s	Be aware of your people and behavior or productivity changes.		
s	Be lenient when unintentional, but fix problem.		
s	Punish to max when intentional.		
s	Promote examples as deterrent.		
s	Encourage self-report.		
s	Use tiered approach for permissions, and let people know they are being monitored.		
s	Publish the top 10; let people know you are watching.		
s	Textbook and reality. There is a difference.		
s	Oversight.		
s	Scrutiny.		
S	Audit logs.		

(*Continued*)

Table 5.2 How *Information Technology Specialists* Mitigate Risk to Insider Threat to Organization, Thereby Enhancing Resilience

CATEGORY	CORE CATEGORY = C, OR SUB-CATEGORY = S	CHECKOFF YES	CHECKOFF NO
C	**F. Follow Rules and Guidelines for Information Security Protection and Implement for Prevention**	**Checkoff Yes**	**Checkoff No**
s	Set in place, and ensure permissions are followed. For example, file permission, file structure, and data collection.		
s	Comply with common access card management protocols.		
s	Set physical rules; lock away timers.		
S	Follow rules for permissions and pin resets.		
s	Ensure two-chain events are followed.		
s	Compare identification to individual, in person to verify authenticity before a pin reset.		
s	Disallow a person access.		
s	Build in network safeguard to screen connections.		
s	Train basic user [ensure].		
s	Ensure basic users do not have root access.		
s	Work with people who spill to fix problems.		
s	Textbook: Make sure security controls are in place and being aware/conscious.		
s	Work with people in process of cleanup.		
s	Clean up spills (web, email, other).		
s	Use software to block access to certain internet sites.		
s	Build encryptions into laptops.		
s	Tag or meta-tag documents.		
s	Be wary of updates and patching when violations occur.		
s	Keep look out for changes, or user behavior, or unexpected network changes.		
s	Enforce policy changes.		
s	Rely on technology.		
C	**G. Apply Subject Matter Expertise to Monitor Threats or Detect Compromise**	**Checkoff Yes**	**Checkoff No**
s	Actively monitor in person.		
s	Spot-check bags; understand what people are taking home.		
s	Use electronic monitoring and screening systems.		
s	Use different monitoring systems.		

(*Continued*)

Table 5.2 (*Continued*) How *Information Technology Specialists* Mitigate Risk to Insider Threat to Organization, Thereby Enhancing Resilience

CATEGORY	CORE CATEGORY = C, OR SUB-CATEGORY = S	CHECKOFF YES	CHECKOFF NO
S	Cross-reference and pool resources with regard to alerts.		
S	Experience of understanding of what employee is doing in the system.		
S	Audit logs.		
S	Centralize approved process of system administrators.		
S	Block at source IP, and email when identified as risk.		
S	Be aware and conscious.		
S	Use analytic tools, some automated. Noted money limitation.		
C	**H. Prevent User Error**	**Checkoff Yes**	**Checkoff No**
S	Look out for best interest of employee from doing something in advert.		
S	Put together things to mitigate. Such as development process, rules and policy.		
S	Use phased approach to implement new security requirements.		
S	Implement three strikes policy for information assurance [cybersecurity violations].		
S	Ensure system administrators receive extra training on threat of abuse.		
S	Worry about security controls.		
S	Conduct prevention training.		
S	Provide a frequently asked questions page for users.		
S	Conduct more vulnerability scans with better equipment and updated software.		
S	More documentation for the user to access.		
C	**I. Respond to, and Recover from Incidents**	**Checkoff Yes**	**Checkoff No**
S	Clean up spills.		
S	Work with people.		
S	Follow through alerts, go through fully to end state, follow up, action, and countermeasure.		
S	Conduct training as part of response.		
S	Capture lessons learned.		
S	Identify the bad actions, and appropriate administrative action.		
S	Explain policy. Know the policy, so you can explain it.		

(*Continued*)

Table 5.2 (*Continued*)   How *Information Technology Specialists* Mitigate Risk to Insider Threat to Organization, Thereby Enhancing Resilience

CATEGORY	CORE CATEGORY = C, OR SUB-CATEGORY = S	CHECKOFF YES	CHECKOFF NO
S	Explain correlations between an action and potential threat.		
S	Provide security incident reports and how the problem was solved.		
S	Report back to originating unit incident findings.		
S	Share lessons learned to prevent repeating errors.		
C	**J. Develop Self and Apply Critical Thinking Practice**	**Checkoff Yes**	**Checkoff No**
S	Understand risk.		
S	Hands-on application.		
S	Get new training to keep up with emerging issues.		
S	Worry about security controls (repeat).		
S	Interpret and explain procedures.		
C	**K. Get the Job Done**	**Checkoff Yes**	**Checkoff No**
S	Engineers often get the back end and must work in reverse.		
S	Get the job done at all costs, with less money, and less assets, because we always have. (This will not apply to all organizations-the organizational ethos/culture will drive this.)		
S	Some technology specialists will intentionally let things fail, so that management will listen and prioritize budget.		
S	Integrity of information.		
C	**L. Advisor to Management**	**Checkoff Yes**	**Checkoff No**
S	Use expertise to give insight.		
S	IT experts are relied upon by management.		
S	Different types of IT specialist may advise on various aspects. (Identify within house skillsets/backgrounds.)		
S	A certified information systems security professional may serve as interpreter to management. Managers should get to know their staff's certifications.		
S	Make it easier for management to grasp the complex technical.		

As indicated in Tables 5.1 and 5.2, there are many ways that managers and information technology specialists mitigate risk. I separated the next section into two parts to describe how managers and then how information technology specialists mitigate risk to insider threat to organization, thereby enhancing organizational resilience. Although there were some similarities even overlapping in different core categories, their roles were also distinctly different. The emerging themes, five for manager and seven for information technology specialist, are listed here, as summarized from the previous tables.

1. The following five emergent themes were identified overall for managers:
   - Extensive training emphasis
   - Application of management practice, including textbook ideal vs. actual
   - Develop and follow business rules and guidelines
   - Storytelling; tell stories that transcend and interpret cyber-physical reality
   - Perform managerial policing actions

Whereas every participant of my original research on insider threat emphasized training, the value of this training was emphasized even more by managers. There is a perception that most organizations lack in this area. Absent are the extensive ongoing training programs for all employees, instead relying on yearly training that might be a couple of hours at the most and briefly cover insider threat. Given emergent threats, including human behavior and changing technology, training and awareness needs to be elevated substantively.

Unfortunately, many businesses and organizations may not have established any training program, let alone an indoctrination or annual training requirement; this is high risk. For those who currently have a limited training program, at minimum, supplementary notices and issue specific training can be provided on an ad hoc basis if an increased threat is identified to that organizational entity. However, executive leadership support would likely be needed, and this could be dependent on the knowledge or emphasis of specific governance support executives in response to the knowledge of current threat awareness.

In the practical application for managers, interesting themes emerged in my original research between an ideal state of management, and the reality of a very busy manager and how more urgent tasks could easily drive prioritization. Essentially, a contrast between the practical applications versus what management should be doing is based on textbook ideology. Limitations of staffing capability, or lack of core knowledge, could prevent application of textbook best practices in some circumstances.

Developing business rules and guidelines, and forecasting for the future seemed to be a common ideal theme for managers. Another important theme that emerged was the important role of meaningful organizational storytelling that transcends the cyber-physical realities of the workplace. Storytelling seemed to be a tool of prevention, as well as lessons learned, and consequence and conclusion. Managers are often expected to wear several hats in their policing work to ensure that employees are doing what they should be doing on multiple levels, including oversight of personnel, physical environment, and information systems. For managers, there is a greater emphasis on formal punishment for intentional security violations and awareness of the consequences. I shift now to the emergent theme of the information technology specialist.

2. The following seven emergent themes were identified for information technology specialists overall:
   - Follow rules and guidelines
   - Apply subject matter expertise to monitor threats or detect compromise
   - Prevent user error
   - Directly respond to, and recover from incidents including on-the-spot retraining
   - Develop self and apply critical thinking practice
   - Get the job done
   - Be an advisor to management

Information technology specialists are computer system–function focused. More than the manager, they are focused on the actual user of the computer system. By focusing on the user and their potential behavior, there can be effective prevention efforts to eliminate potential user error. These early detection prevention measures start, in part, with a focus on user training as well as technology-based controls to prevent errors.

However, despite prevention approaches, because of the growth of technology devices and varied platforms, the constant changes in technology create a significant amount of work and frustration for the information technology specialist to stay current. The changing technologies, the introduction of new risk or newly discovered vulnerabilities, and the implications to the information technology specialist, the user, and the organization at large can be challenging to stay on top of cybersecurity.

Information assurance is challenging, especially more so if staffing/hiring numbers are not adequate. Gaps in hiring create increased risk. Applying subject matter expertise is absolutely necessary, but for continuous improvement and in order for this subject matter expert to be successful, they also need the support of organizational governance with an active risk management framework and process, and current tools for monitoring of the computer system, in addition to in-person monitoring.

Cleaning up spills for the information technology specialist is time consuming because of the level of research and detailed corrections that are typically needed. Taking the time to think strategically can also be difficult because of the day-to-day challenges to get the job done. Essentially, it is difficult to step outside of the trenches and see the larger battlefield, especially with defense activities. The information technology specialist needs to continue with hands-on application, as well as ongoing training to keep up with emerging issues. However, regardless of resources, the information technology specialist is expected to get the job done, but money remains a big challenge.

For the information technology specialist, accountability after the fact remains important, and policies regarding consequences should be enforced, along with prevention training. Even information technology specialists with elevated privileges could make errors, the virtuous and wicked insider, though well-intended action may have been the motivator. This demonstrates a more empathetic personal association with computer users and unintended insider threat.

As an advisor, the information technology specialist could be useful if the right questions are asked by management; or within the risk management process, the early detection of particular issues could be advised swiftly. These subject matter experts as resources may be overlooked because of hierarchical blinders. Many information technology specialists will come from different educational tracks and may have more technical certifications than degrees. It is useful for their managers to get to know their qualifications, including if they are a Certified Information Systems Security Professional,[1] which is a difficult qualification that demonstrates a higher level of expertise.

From a contrasting standpoint between managers and information technology specialists, managers were more focused on strategic management and policing, but spent less time on spill cleanup and on-the-spot corrections than the information technology specialist, whose focus is at a more granular level. Funding was a concern for both managers and information technology specialists; both identify a recognition of the need for monetary investment and prioritization up front, not at the end or simply in response to an incident. Creating up-to-date training was also important to both roles, as well as making sure those requirements weren't just checked off, but were more comprehensively understood by employees. Due to technological advances and emerging threats, training once a year was marginal with persistent ongoing awareness deemed necessary. There was an intrinsic value of knowledge and awareness of actual organizational incidents. Recognizing that some specifics might need to be left out for security reasons, but that knowing the causal action, the impact, and consequences on multiple levels would be invaluable and potentially an ethics or fear appeal in the efforts of prevention.

Highlighting these errors can be culturally difficult for organizations. Many managers and/or leaders do not want to air their dirty laundry or showcase these failures; however, I believe that it can be done in a way that reporting these compromises is an opportunity to increase resiliency. If failures are not socialized, they are bound to be repeated. The assessment or lessons learned, especially drawn from potential insider threat behavior, can in turn showcase corrective measures and promotes employee accountability. When managers do recognize the organizational emphasis, they may increase the prioritization of increased cybersecurity training in the workplace within their span of control.

Accountability by senior leadership, including executive governance structures for their people in awareness and training as well as compliance, was an area that was explored by both managers and information technology specialists. Creating specific linkages to evaluations, rather than in general terms, is a potential solution; not just simply in vague terms, but in very specific terms. Routine technology security training could reduce risk, especially with emerging trends.

Further investigative capabilities, essential audit capabilities, also need to be established by organizations outside of the role of manager and information technology specialist in order to enhance resilience, similar to that of an investigative general. For example, in the 1980s the role of the inspector general in the U.S. Army changed from that of strict compliance to a new emphasis on compliance-systemic inspection methodology that focused on causes that ultimately allowed for errors or omissions in policy to be addressed.[2] While this may not seem like a huge revelation, the reality is that the policies behind insider threat have often been absent, with those employees who are part of the problem, auditing themselves. As previously described no one in an organization is immune from being an insider threat. Recently, the U.S. Department of Defense announced that they were beginning cybersecurity reports audit, basically examining how they were auditing and reporting on the topic in order to (1) summarize cybersecurity reports issued and testimonies made by their audit community and the GAO in the prior year in order to (2) identify gaps in audit coverage based on the five functions of the National Institute of Standards and Technology Cybersecurity Framework, and then to (3) identify cybersecurity risk areas for defense management to address.[3] While this won't apply to all organizations, there are many businesses that are contracted to do work for the Department of Defense, and it could impact them with demonstrating their cybersecurity posture. Additionally, the example shows that organizations should also consider doing a similar assessment to mitigate their risk posture. The gaps, or the deltas, are very important to identify, especially with ongoing changes in technology and persistent insider threat.

5.2 Managerial Approaches

Active managerial oversight, employee behavior observation, and development and adherence mechanisms to policy are required in order to become more resilient against insider threat. Infamous insider threat cases like Edward Snowden might have been prevented if there had been increased pre-hiring scrutiny as well as active and very direct managerial oversight and employee behavior observation by the contracting firm that hired Snowden. Although immediate action was taken to fire him, the damage had played out and even became a movie because of his bizarre and scripted method. This insider threat was not just damaging to the company's client, but it was damaging to the contracting firm's existence itself. This was big. Not only did Snowden place many of the U.S. intelligence methods at public scrutiny, but he also placed the contracting firm who hired him at great risk. The contracting firm could have very well collapsed because of one individual's ideology on how to manage something he did not fundamentally agree with. Unfortunately, in this case I don't think that training would have created a different outcome, however monitoring and detailed screening for unauthorized downloading devices might have.

If the company had not been as resilient in light of this damaging situation, and had Snowden known that he might be responsible for 20,000 people losing their jobs, would this have appealed to Snowden's ethics? Probably not. The fear of punishment certainly had no bearing on this individual. The narcissistic appeal certainly was a big influence on Snowden; however, reports indicate that he did not earn money for the film production, but the infamy might have been payment enough.[4] Snowden's father served an honorable lifetime career in the U.S. Coast Guard, and his son's behavior certainly potentially overshadowed this contribution.

5.2.1 Training Emphasis

Organizations have to balance the cost of training against the overall return on investment of the training. This isn't new. Training is expensive, the cost of the training itself, and the cost of the individual to take the training. However, not training can be equally expensive. Sometimes there is caution that if an employee gets too much training, their value increases and they will leave. On the flip side, if you are not training, you also risk a lot as well. Finding the right balance for training is important for the benefit of the organization. Creating retention initiatives may offset potential loss. According to security managers, the training seems to never be enough and needs to consistently be refreshed. Incorporating cybersecurity into core competencies and an ongoing competency being delivered through virtual means, as well as in-person means, can provide some risk reduction. Exploring various innovative delivery methods of training is also ideal. Training in information technology security awareness may be thought of in terms of marketing: How to get the right message to the workforce.

Reminders of requirements can be pushed out now electronically, but they need to be read and comprehended for the message to be received. Not many people understand the nature of human behavior and their role as a potential unintended insider threat. Into the future, new and innovative ways to train need to be sought out, accountability must be incorporated, and users need to understand in practice what to do and what not to do both on and off the network.

In my first professional job in the private sector, the staff was invited to monthly training lunches. These luncheons were voluntary and not part of my regular job, but everyone in the organization was invited. As a more junior member of the staff, this incentivized me to go. I would get a fantastic lunch and earn valuable knowledge with training certification. In this first business job, we were still using hard copy file-a-deck systems in my branch, yet there was still an occurrence of insider threat that I experienced and my failure to monitor properly. I worked for a reputable collection agency, and my administrative job was to review the phone logs of the collectors, as well as pick up the file-a-deck cards with accounts and distribute them for collections. In reviewing the telephone logs, I failed and missed a repeatable long-distance call to a country in Africa. Not familiar with long-distance calling digits, I thought it was a code of some sort and not a logged call. The company I worked for got a whopping long-distance bill in the thousands of dollars (because long-distance calling was very expensive in the 1980s). Apparently, a collector had been making calls to her mother in Africa from the work line. The company decided not to fire the employee, or seek legal action, instead they allowed the employee to continue working with increased monitoring so she could pay them back. I learned a valuable lesson about monitoring, and assumptions as well. When I saw this code, I should have brought it up to the attention of my manager to assess the risk. In my position, I had monitored the phone calls, but when an anomaly came up, at that point in my career, I did not critically think well enough, and in reflection really giving the illusion of properly monitoring due to lack of awareness and training. This lesson learned is still relevant today in information technology security. If anomalies are brushed aside without investigation, the illusion of monitoring continues to exist.

5.2.2 Practice in Application

Managers of information technology security need to be managers and not just workers. They need to connect with the organizational structure points to bring about change, support the risk management process, and engage with senior leadership and executive governance. If a risk management framework is not in place, they can help to drive the creation of one through the chief information officer (CIO), or the chief information security officer (CISO). Although results alone from these traditional risk assessments may not be enough. One of the purposes behind this book is to look more closely at human behavior as part of the insider threat. The risk assessments scope can be limited and is not necessarily the be-all end-all solution but can certainly be an indicator, and in certain circumstances assist in having more data to contribute to more effective risk informed decision making. A special publication from NIST 800-30, rev.1 on risk assessment cautions that assessments are not always precise measurements and have limitations of methodology, tools, and techniques; there is also a fair amount of subjectivity, quality, and trust limitations of the data along with interpretation and the skill levels of those who are conducting the assessments.[5] That being said, having a risk management framework is useful.

Managers need to aim to work strategically, promote transparency, interoperability, and accountability including monitoring of work and behavior. Managers need to apply their skill set and be forward thinking, and they need to ask more questions from those who work for them, including "What questions am I not asking that I should be?"

Managers should have the time to read new books, new articles, reflect on the past lessons learned, and attend or conduct panels on topics in their area of expertise. However, in reality, their time can be prioritized in a less-optimal state—senior leadership needs to prioritize this attention to the professional development of managers of information technology security and the ability for them to manage more strategically. Remaining current, knowing their workplace environment, and being forward leaning to how the workplace should be changing is invaluable.

5.2.3 Develop and Follow Business Rules and Guidelines

An important role for the manager in developing business rules is also to know when to say no, to say it, and mean it. Controls that technologically can be put into place, but are not, should be seriously considered along with simply not establishing unsafe storage, file shares, protocols, or platforms where information security cannot be verified. If a system needs to be redesigned, and or additional safeguards established, then the manager should be able to push for that and be a hands-on participant, when necessary. Managers should understand the need to identify IT security rules and what procedures are needed, create guidelines, and then train and reinforce through testing and on-the-spot checks. When possible ensure that safeguards are built into network connections. Lessons learned are an excellent tool for the manager of information technology security to review what occurred, and to develop new or modify existing business rules and guidelines. To do so managers need to keep their head above water and be focused strategically to be a visionary for cybersecurity and reduction of insider threat, to align resources, and to get his/her team to the end goal of mitigating the risk against the organization both inside and out. Ensuring that key cybersecurity positions are in place is a good place to start. The cybersecurity workforce is much broader than most people think.

A good open-source resource for the manager to examine the potential for positions in their organizational workforce is the National Initiative for Cybersecurity Education (NICE) Cybersecurity Workforce Framework.[6] This framework was developed with the intent to be applied by not just government, but also private and academia.

It can assist organizations to assess their cybersecurity workforce, which can lend itself to mitigating risks that have been created by gaps of missing particular key positions. Seven cybersecurity workforce categories are grouped and include common cybersecurity functions, they are: Oversee and Govern; Operate and Maintain; Investigate; Collect and Operate; Analyze; Security Provision; and Protect and Defend. Within these categories, there are several distinct areas of cybersecurity work functions identified, where specific tasks can be mapped to these functions, as well as the knowledge, skills, and abilities required. For a manager, the forward-leaning aspect might be to do a thorough assessment of the organization and any missing key positions, any functional positions that are missing will need to be further developed.

5.2.4 Storytelling: Tell Stories That Transcend and Interpret Cyber-Physical Reality

Storytelling can be achieved in a narrative, but also through pictures and images. Stories can become part of a culture because they are real stories that are thrust upon them, per say, without warning. They might be shocking stories found in the media for example. Male politicians are really good about being caught up in ethics scandals usually involving another woman who is not their wife. Anthony Weiner, now former U.S. Congressional House Representative from New York is a classic example of storytelling the "sexting scandal."

Weiner's inappropriate digitally based behavior, which included images of himself in boxer shorts with an erection, forced his resignation from a seat in Congress, later losing a mayoral bid, losing his marriage to Huma Abedin (Hillary Clinton's aide), and getting him a federal prison sentence after his numerous sexting scandals through social media like Twitter, Facebook, and via email—ultimately his final sexting scandal to a 15-year-old girl. After this report about the underaged girl surfaced, Weiner proactively turned himself into the FBI and under a plea bargain plead guilty to a single charge of transferring obscene material to a minor, rather than potentially facing higher level child pornography charges. Weiner is now serving a 21-month sentence in federal prison sentence and will be a registered sex offender. His exploits included asking the girl to engage in sexually explicit performance via Skype and Snapchat.[7]

Cascading consequences in the seizure of his electronic devices that were owned by Weiner and his wife was that they contained emails related to a separate Hillary Clinton election scandal. This prompted the FBI director James Comey to reopen an investigation, a move that Hillary Clinton later attributed to one of the reasons she did not win the election because of the critical timing, which occurred 11 days before the 2016 presidential election.[8]

Associations matter. Labels may be inferred upon an organization by association of the people in the story, with their various affiliations. Stories that are counter to the culture of the organization will get criticized and rationalized. Claims that individuals are not representative of the organization, which an individual is acting outside of organizational norms. Those acting outside of the norms can expect to quickly become alienated. Weiner resigned from Congress, but his bad behavior continued, despite the general public typically being forgiving of politicians' indiscretions when they are remorseful. Hillary Clinton continued to keep Huma Abedin in her employment, and with the ongoing sexting and election scandals, doing so likely contributed to her election loss; however, it was not just about the election emails, it was also about the judgment about Huma Abedin who continued to stay with her spouse, with repeated transgressions, and remained close to Hillary Clinton as an advisor. This too may have contributed to the election loss. It is possible she was empathetic toward Abedin, but ties should have been severed years before.

5.2.5 Performing Policing Actions

Managers need to monitor and ensure policing actions are taken. This monitoring can be done through both human and technology. Employees should be aware and informed that they are subject to this monitoring as part of their employment, within the scope of the law. Managers should assess the work environment to determine how best to conduct particular monitoring, within limits of the law including being compliant with Civil Rights laws. Electronic monitoring and screening systems as well as in-person spot-checks should all be used for proper handling and managing of information. The behavior typologies addressed earlier in this book may be used to compare against for potential mitigation of employee risk. A manager of information security needs to wear multiple hats that include personnel, physical, and information systems as part of cybersecurity to be successful.

Awareness of an organization's changing risk landscape will be critical as well. A first step would be to establish an understanding of the risk landscape. This is not necessarily a classified type of document and could be assembled quite easily with an interdisciplinary team to focus on the issue. Technology should be leveraged as part of the monitoring solutions. Close attention should be paid to behavior and progress of work stages. This does not mean that some leniency can't be applied; it can, but if errors are made, individuals should receive on-the-spot retraining as part of mediation, especially when not intentional. However, continually repeating the behavior won't create additional security within the organization.

Establishing methods for security reporting including insider threat reporting is beneficial, including self-reporting options. Errors will happen; we have discussed how frequently they can happen. Data should be collected for scrutiny and auditability. Examples of selected insider threat situations should be promoted as a deterrent for others to repeat similar behavior. A quick hitter could be to publish the top 10 violation categories, tiers of punishment, and/or actions in order to let people know that they are being monitored. Most employees do not understand how they might contribute to allowing threat to enter the organization and do not likely internalize that they are part of the insider threat problem. There is an opportunity for all employees to increase organizational resilience and become the gestalt of organizational resilience effectively reducing enterprise risk.

5.3 Information Technology Specialist Approaches

In 1999, a well-known toy company produced 12-inch action figures of Coast Guardsman. They were in standard action figure presentation boxes with a clear cellophane view, and many jokes circulated about what accessories would come with each particular rate (job type). For example, the aviators would come with a set of sunglasses and a pretty sidekick. However, what is the most memorable to me about the jokes, and in part the culture, was that the information technology specialists' figures were speculated to come with a completely sealed box, with no cellophane window, would never be able to leave the box, and no one would be allowed to see the work they were doing.

The reality is that information technology specialists are generally quite busy all the time, but the general workforce probably knows much less about what they do and how they do it. When tech support is needed, they are a hot commodity and the rescuers of the day. What has generally struck me over the years in working with these specialists is their genuine love for the work that they perform, yet how quiet they are about their work. At times, their technical expertise can be invisible to the less-technical computer user, and instead they need to literally step outside the box more to showcase their work through awareness products and strategic interdisciplinary communications. An emphasis should be on current and future investment, and not waiting until they must work directly with an employee to fix problems, or in worse cases fix actual spills to minimize damage after a compromise has occurred.

5.3.1 Approach to Following Rules and Guidelines

A distinction between managers and specialists is that rather than develop and follow business rules and guidelines, the information technology specialist is primarily focused on following and implementing the rules and guidelines for information security protection and prevention. Most information specialists will have elevated privileges within an organization, so following the rules should be continually reinforced especially as many privileged users have the ability to side step controls. When violations occur, these are reported, but the assessment of trends as well as punitive measures, are typically left to management. Specialists tend to focus on retraining and preventing future rule violations for the users.

5.3.2 Apply Subject Matter Expertise to Monitor Threats or Detect Compromise

The information technology specialist is busy and often reliant on technology and specific event management software to keep a look out for changes, or a digital footprint of users' behavior or unexpected network changes, as well as logging changes that occur. They must make sure that security controls are in place, as well as monitor those controls. Understanding what a network looks like and how devices should look when working within established rules is also a focus.

For example, if a large amount of data suddenly is exported, and this is an anomalous behavior for a particular user, or system, then the information specialist will have to quickly investigate and identify why this has occurred, and if it is a proper transaction. As discussed in the OPM breach of 2015, often legitimate software can be used to perform illegal activities; understanding how to recognize the differences takes focused vigilance. Training should be ongoing and continuous for these specialists, setting budgets to properly train, as well as enabling professional conferences is ideal. Cross-training in personal and physical security is also beneficial, though not always common practice.

5.3.3 Prevent User Error

Prevention is the key word here. Up-front efforts can make a big difference including controls that prevent user error to begin with. This means blocking access to particular websites and limiting user privileges to prevent the modifications of systems or data. Ensuring employees understand what the proper policy is can mean the difference between elevated risk and lower mitigated risk. Training is also central to prevention, as I have discussed. Along with proper hiring, proper termination protocols should also be followed. All types of employees are tempted to remove information that likely does not belong to them. Just because an employee created a product or data while in employment or has access to particular data certainly does not mean the exiting employee can take it with them. Far from it, information and data are property of the organization that paid someone to create it, unless that person received special permission that might include copy write or expressed permission. In one case similar to this, I was contacted because an employee was insisting that they needed technical support to download multiple documents and was demanding that tech support assist them in doing so. The controls were in place so the employee could not remove the data, and the information technology specialist knew he could not remove the data but wanted a higher level of policy backup. I was able to point to the policy that prohibited the removal. The employee who was departing was not going on bad terms, but erroneously thought he could take his work with him.

5.3.4 Directly Respond to and Recover from Incidents Including On-the-Spot Retraining

Managing cleanups can be time consuming and depending on scale could be more of a surge response with additional resources being allocated depending on the scope. Because of the redundant nature of the internet and social media sharing, it can be difficult to remove information that is unauthorized for release; however, best efforts still must be made to do so. Retraining can provide reduction so that user errors can be reduced. Ensuring that users understand how their action has direct correlation to potential threats is ideal.

Processes should be in place to facilitate incident response and recovery, as well as documenting the incidents so that appropriate follow-up analysis can be made, and ideally best practices shared. In circumstances when patches and updates are required, the information technology specialist should pay extra attention to ensure a trusted source and proper supply chain security is assured. Again, privileged users are at higher risk for forcing overrides and searching for patching on the web without going to a trusted source is high risk, because the threats are looming on the web, simply waiting for that privileged user to grab them, and open the door to the network.

5.3.5 Develop Self and Apply Critical Thinking Practice

To continue self-development and applying critical-thinking practices, it is increasingly important to keep up with emergent trends and learning more about cascading consequences and acceptance of risk to having a particular level of security controls. An information technology specialist should learn about their organization as well, looking inside, as well as how it looks from the outside in. In part this is what this book is about, bringing additional insight into human behavior, and the overlapping responsibilities of all employees to protect against insider threat, all types—the virtuous, wicked, vengeful, and malicious. It is imperative that information technology specialists never stop learning, never stop training, never stop applying and communicating their findings. Critical analysis, critical thinking, and innovation will be needed and highly valued well into the future; however, it is not just to apply processes. Increasingly, it is about challenging the status quo and ensuring that conducting enterprise-wide risk assessments are properly assessed and the risks are mitigated with high integrity.

5.3.6 Get the Job Done

The job does need to get done, however, a balance between necessary security and acceptable risk must happen. Technology security is expensive, but there are solutions that can be applied that incorporate changes without layering solutions on top of broken and old processes. Assembling the correct stakeholders at the correct point in a design, and/or acquisition is important. Fixing security issues after the initial design or build concept is more expensive and time consuming; reverse engineering happens, but it is not ideal. Having the correct system engineers and experts on the front end of a project needs to occur. Almost all acquisitions should be assessed for potential information technology interdependencies.

5.3.7 Special Advisor to Management

Within any field there are many levels and layers of talent. Identifying the experts who are change agents that are experts in their fields, regardless of the level in which they reside within the organization is important. This expertise needs to be used by managers and executives. Managers should get to know what the credentials are of their staffs and how particular experts might be able to help facilitate in the translation of complex technical problems into meaningful mental models.

5.4 Practical Mental Models Continued

The following mental models are beneficial in assessing mitigation of risk and enhancing organizational resilience. Thus far, I have introduced five mental models of insider threat. I continue to unfold the remaining four mental models that are all aspects of a grounded theory of insider cyber threat. The previous chapters have continued to build upon your understanding of this definition and conceptualization with very practical application, thus creation of a greater depth of understanding of insider threat, assessment, and mitigation of risk.

5.4.1 Mental Model (Aspect 6)—Storytelling to Achieve Information Security Awareness Culture

I call the next model *Aspect 6,* which is *a grounded theory aspect in the value of transparent organizational storytelling in shaping and understanding a new organizational information technology security aware culture.* Storytelling can help to shape an organizational culture. Deliberate storytelling, that is transparent, to assist with the learning process, to make real connections could create a deeper meaning to the listener. The sharing of stories that have been written or created within the organization can be helpful. Some organizations may be able to reshape their narrative more easily than others.

Legacy organizations, which could potentially have a less flexible culture, more rigid managers or employees, may be more resistant to storytelling. If an organization or agency bureau is newer, and employees have been assembled from a diverse background, it might be easier to reshape with these meaningful information technology security awareness stories. Most employees who have been in a newer organization have had to adapt, are more likely to come from a diverse background, and I would expect this diversity and flexibility can be very useful.

However, newer organizations and businesses may also struggle to have a common culture, because it can take some time to integrate into a culture to begin with. Organizations with high leadership turnover could also experience some difficulty in creating useful stories that are authentic. Authenticity matters. I'm going to repeat that: authenticity matters, really. No one likes to be manipulated or treated with insincerity, and many of us have a keen aptitude for detecting this. If the meanings and stories are not sincere, it might take longer to reshape that culture, or worse yet, create a counterculture because of the insincere messaging.

If you were to take a moment to think about some catch phrases that people might say to you in passing, these are stories that are potentially shaping a culture or counterculture. Reflect on if these are the right messages that should be shared; is there an opportunity cost to these messages? How different messaging might be incentivized is certainly an option. For example, if you want your leaders to be sincere and care about their people, this means they need to stop and listen to their answers when asked a question. Even stop to say thank you once in a while.

If an organizational culture has been built upon having to balance technology advancements, privacy, and other sensitivities and is technology centric, it might be easier to change the storytelling and strategic messaging. Technology is adaptive and ever changing, and those people immersed in it can sometimes see how they need to get on that bus, or the bus is going to leave without them. Sometimes it takes a story about the bus leaving to realize that there really is a bus. Walking papers, unfortunately, tell a more severe story, and typically you will be locked out of the bus depot before you realize the bus is gone.

The bottom line is this—storytelling also needs to be authentic, or it will be dismissed by counter stories. Telling transparent stories may be difficult but is necessary and part of strategic communications. Also listening to the current culture can help organizational storytellers identify what has to be changed, what will be more difficult to be changed, and what approach needs to be taken. Sometimes old stories need to be left alone and replaced by new ones, rather than being directed for cancellation. The following is an example of this.

Every four years or so, the top leadership in the U.S. Coast Guard changes. This can be a good thing, but it has also more recently caused some very odd messaging showcasing that a culture can be significantly bigger than one leader's direction of thou-shalt-not. For background, historically the Coast Guard military workforce has referred to themselves as Coasties, I assume because a lot of the work traditionally was conducted on the coasts of the United States, such as search and rescue. Friends and families often refer to their loved one in the U.S. Coast Guard in a familiar way as a Coastie.

However, strategic messaging was directed down around 2010 to say that this was not a proper term, and that Coasties should not be used; instead, Coastguardsman was now the proper term to be used. Not only that change, but everyone should refer to themselves and each other as shipmates. Of course not everyone had served on a ship, but that was beside the point; shipmate was quickly used in both positive and negative ways, and sometimes you weren't quite sure which way it was being used. There is that authenticity again. Suddenly, "Good morning, shipmate," was not always taken in a positive way. Also, the term "man" did not represent a high part of the workforce, and the internalization of Coastie couldn't just be removed. It was like saying to a member of the Marine Corps, that they stopped being a Marine. Four years after the direction, the new commandant blessed that it was just fine to refer to oneself in many different ways, which could include Coastie. Indeed all was well again in the world. The terms Coastguardsman and shipmate did not go away, but the historical was no longer shunned.

An example of reshaping an organizational culture in the face of privacy violations occurred just days after apologetic Facebook CEO provided testimony before U.S. Congress. Essentially, Facebook responded very quickly with commercials where they summarized what the organization had initially done correctly, how they went off course such as by allowing false news and user information to be used, how the company is getting back on course for the benefit of the consumer experience and protection of their data, and getting back to their authentic purpose—one of feeling connected. It was a very good targeted messaging; of course, Facebook has some top talent in many areas. It used cute video stories from its users, and the messaging appeared to appeal to internal ethics and was authentically portrayed by the CEO. This messaging was of course focused external to the company, but the reality is all of the employees are also highly likely to be users of their social media service.

In a contrasting example, after the terrorist attacks on U.S. soil in 2001, the U.S. government had to create massive reorganization to try to change a culture that had not been focused well enough on information sharing. Still there remained well-documented information-sharing struggles, in part, I assess because there was simply a reshuffle of people between old and new agencies with the same type of culture often counter to information sharing. Of course, there are times when well-established laws do not allow such information sharing, so there are legal, policy, and process barriers that were not entirely removed in this historical reorganization of the U.S. government. However, the massive reorganization also sent a message of rebranding and getting back to what government should have been doing by protecting the homeland to begin with.

*5.4.2 Mental Model (Aspect 7)—Communication
          Chain of Compelling Interpretation*

The next mental model I call *Aspect 7,* which is *a grounded theory aspect of interpretation; the chain of compelling interpretation needed within an organization from the technology specialist, to the manager, to the senior leader for effective organizational decision making and achieving resilience.* This chain of interpretation is about communications. In order to convey meaning, a manager should be able to understand what their technical specialists mean by their word selection, and be able to relay that to senior decision makers in a meaningful way, the intent and how this impacts the larger organizational system. There is an element of storytelling to this, in meaningful terms. Compelling information and stories are necessary for attention. An information technology specialist, who is not a manager, may have difficulty in creating meaning in the day-to-day language of the senior leadership. This theoretical aspect advocates for having managers grow out of subject matter expertise, as well as having managers grow into the discipline of information technology specialization. In order to enhance organizational resilience, a better understanding and comprehension of the issues are needed. An element of trust is also needed, so that decision makers, even if they do not fully understand the nuts-and-bolts implications, can be assured of cascading consequences that need to be mitigated. This compelling chain would also expand to the employee, who should also be able to communicate with an information technology specialist or a manager surrounding observations, concerns, or best practices.

Recently, I was trying to clarify a process among a technical sponsor of an IT acquisition, a disability technical compliance coordinator, and an organizational acquisition manager, but it was difficult to understand who had primary responsibility because of the word "program," mostly because this is a term used by different experts in different fields. Telling me the program was responsible meant nothing, since all of those responsible were part of a different program. Ultimately, there was a great confusion about who was responsible for a particular review function in the acquisition process for a technical acquisition. Simply saying the program was responsible basically left room for a lot of interpretation, and key elements to be dropped, with potential high risk of non-compliance of federal law. Fortunately, I was able to clarify the term and address the change process to be more specific to mitigate future risk.

5.4.3 Mental Model (Aspect 8)—Ideological Textbook Approach vs. Reality Constraints

Aspect 8 is a grounded theory aspect of managerial textbook versus reality. There are many textbook-type approaches to information security management; however, the reality is that there are other factors, such as an abundance of never-ending work, that can get in the way of keeping current and implementing these potentially best practices. The information technology specialist, the manager, and senior leadership should be aware of these limitations. This can be interpreted as a reality versus ideological textbook state. There can be mismatch of expectations at various hierarchical levels.

In addition to the eight aspects already introduced, during my original study, two additional mental models emerged (*Aspect 9* and *Aspect 10*) from my reflectivity after I had developed the consolidated conceptualization of Theory 1, a grounded theory of insider cybersecurity threat to organization (which is depicted in the final chapter of this book).

5.4.4 Mental Model (Aspect 9)—Core Competency in Information Technology Security

Aspect 9 is a grounded theory aspect of core competency in information technology security; the need to revisit core competency theory and human resource process from pre-hiring, to hiring, and continued employment accountability. As discussed earlier in this book, the information security organizational culture is becoming so much a part of a regular function in the performance of a job, which needs to be looked at as a basic core competency like reading and writing. Reading, writing, and cybersecurity; there are huge risks to not having a cyber-savvy workforce—well beyond even the basics. Cybersecurity and defense and offense of an organization is complex; however, every potential hire should go through a more rigorous tryout for your varsity team. Regardless of how nice, attractive, disciplined, fit, or qualified someone is, if they can't do the back handspring or meet the varsity football timed shuttle run, they shouldn't make your team.

Cybersecurity training can make someone more employable if they do not possess the skills; however, that extra training investment has to happen at the beginning of employment, and certainly not six months later. After initial training, testing of this knowledge should occur—and routine, but randomly conducted, testing of these competencies.

Individuals may be motivated by different reasons for compliance, and prescreening can potentially help to determine which motivations might be best applied. Earlier research has shown that focusing on either punishments or ethics, depending on individual tendencies, could be effective in threat mitigation in information security; where one or the other could be potentially more effective.[9] The hiring process is an ideal time to assess individuals, but to also be able to generalize if big data is available for the organizational culture.

5.4.5 Mental Model (Aspect 10)—Information Technology Security Accountably and Organizational Resilience

Aspect 10 is *a grounded theory aspect of accountability in information technology security; the connection between performance evaluation on information technology security and organizational resilience.* Without accountability, resilience may be difficult to achieve. Performance-based accountability should be incorporated into all organizational evaluations for employees or surrogate employees. Accountability also means that there should be visibility to incidents, responses, and individual corrective action within the organization, as a best practice. The level of specifics shared will depend on the nature of the organization; the time has come that the organization needs to hold themselves more accountable for critical function of information technology security as a core competency.

Continued employment requirements should also be revisited in each position, at all organizational levels, including at the executive levels. Seniority should never give someone an information technology security insider threat *pass.* Those who resist assessment and applied mitigation measures to reduce the risk of insider threat should be immediately reassessed. No one should be above this accountability. Everyone is an insider threat based on their behavior, ensuring that employees are receptive to monitoring, training, and ongoing testing is a first step to achieving accountability and retaining resilience.

5.5 Theory 1: A Grounded Theory of Insider Cybersecurity Threat to Organization

As you review the digital reconstruction, an analog representation, consider that it is in part the consolidated theoretical conceptualization as well as an attempt to understand and convey both cyber and physical (traditional) insider threat to organization.

The story continues with how the organization can mitigate risk, working with human resources, information technology, physical security, management, leadership, and the employee. External as well as internal defense and offense should also continue. Because of digital archiving, the analog representation originally crafted on my whiteboard has taken a digital form.

Theory 1 is a grounded theory of insider cybersecurity threat to an organization, and listed below as a visual representation in Figure 5.1. In totality, Theory 1 is also comprised of the narratives and categorical responses to the key questions, along with the 10 mental modals, which are all aspects of Theory 1.

Appendix: Best Practice—Practical Knowledge and Practitioner Application

Practical knowledge
- Identify the five emergent themes of the managerial approach.
- Identify the seven emergent themes of the information technology specialist approach.
- Understand the distinctions between approaches of managers and information technology specialists.
- Reflect on the mental models presented and how they link to the insider threat.
- Examine and comprehend Theory 1; a grounded theory of insider cybersecurity threat to an organization.

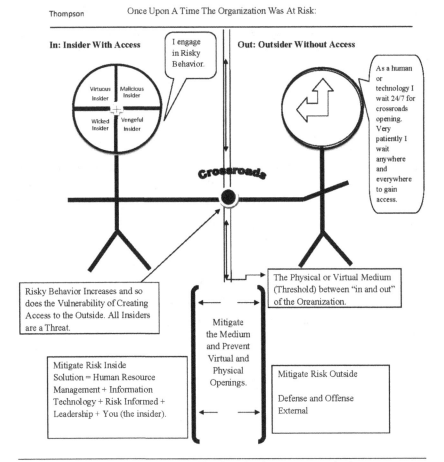

Figure 5.1   Model of a grounded theory of insider cyber threat to an organization.

Practitioner application

- Apply all categorical responses against the Checkoff Yes/No to identify opportunities within your organization; be sure to assess the no answers for potential action.
- Determine the training programs and methods of delivery in your business or organization, assess gaps, then determine how you can launch a more effective and innovative security awareness program.
- Identify the talent you have with both managers and information technology specialists and their credentialing and experience, with the knowledge provided in this chapter, how might

you better use your talent in an advisory capacity against insider threat.

- Identify cultural stories within your organization that fit the direction of the organization, or are counter to the intended culture, and identify how storytelling might reshape the common culture.

Endnotes

1. The CISSP is a registered trademark that is globally recognized credential issued by (ISC)2, developed to meet the highest standard of technical and managerial knowledge. Those who hold the credential are also held to a high ethical standard. Retrieved from https://www.isc2.org/about.
2. Office of the Inspector General on the history of the U.S. Army Inspector General. Note that the updated website from earlier 2013 research was not being read as secure by my browser for the link, so I did not provide it.
3. Inspector General, Department of Defense. Memo dated May 8, 2018 on cybersecurity subject audit. Retrieved from http://www.dodig.mil/reports.html/Article/1517529/.
4. *Snowden* (film) (2016). Produced by Oliver Stone, Screenplay by Oliver Stone and Kieran Fitzgerald. Retrieved from https://en.wikipedia.org/wiki/Snowden_(film).
5. NIST SP 800-30 Rev 1 Guide for Conducting Risk Assessments. Retrieved from www.nist.gov/publications/.
6. NICE Cybersecurity Workforce Framework by the National Institute of Standards and Technology, U.S. Department of Commerce. Retrieved from www.nist.gov/nice/framework.
7. Anthony Weiner gets 21 months in prison for Sexting by Ellie Kaufman and Jean Casarez, CNN. Retrieved from https://www.cnn.com/2017/09/25/politics/anthony-weiner-sentencing/index.html.
8. Hillary Clinton Blames FBI Director for Election Loss, by Amy Chorzick, *New York Times*. Retrieved from https://www.nytimes.com/2016/11/13/us/politics/hillary-clinton-james-comey.html?_r=0.
9. Workman, M. & Gathegi, J. (2006). Punishment and ethics deterrents: A study of insider security contravention. *Journal of American Society for Information Science and Technology*, 58(2), 212–222. doi:10.1002/asi.20474.

BUILDING ORGANIZATIONAL RESILIENCE

A Final Reflection

6.1 Introduction

As I sit down to craft this final chapter, at a haunted historic bed and breakfast near Mystic, Connecticut, I'm struck with the irony that the local internet is open and unsecure. I bang my head against the English oak table, but not too hard because as the story goes there are ghosts that reside here at this inn and I might raise them; I'll try not to raise the spirits, or the hackers. There might also be a sea captain's spirit close by, so I'm told. As for the hacker, well, they are always close by waiting for the human on the inside to make that error. It is very rare for a business entity to not have to fundamentally rely on technology. For example, I know I provided my credit card to hold a reservation for a two-night stay, but how secure was that web portal, now that I know the internet is open? For now, I hope the point of sale system was not directly connected to the open network. I'll be sure to mention it to the inn owner in the morning.

As I look out my window, via the window of my mobile smart-phone, through an incredibly accurate hurricane predictor tracker application,[1] I watch the track line of yet another hurricane barreling up the east coastline. Another year, another natural hazard, and another opportunity to demonstrate increased organizational resilience against all threats, including the human–computer threat—the insider threat. During the crisis of all-hazards events, and other huge global news stories including the news of malicious activities or the latest computer threats, employees tend to click on search engine result links without paying close attention to the legitimacy of the source, which could lead to the entry of malicious activity. Infrastructure and resources can become strained during more regional/local all-hazards events, and malicious actors are waiting to enter through that open threshold, the virtual holes in the fence.

This chapter provides not a full summary, but some additional thoughts for reflection. Ten examples provide illustrative pragmatic-practitioner opportunities of how to build resiliency within an organization. The specific categorical findings and theoretical constructs presented in this book should also be used to inform organizational decision-making approaches. These approaches may include creating more granular risk assessments on specific workplace activities. For an organization, reviewing theories presented in this book, along with assessing comparatively with categorical findings, could be an important part of a larger effort to increase organizational resilience. This review could lead to findings that increase transparency, interoperability, and accountability based on identified challenges and future end states. Organizations must work together to reduce stovepipes that work against each other, an environment where insider threat is sure to flourish. From a risk mitigation standpoint, organizations should seek out individuals with this cyber-physical digital-analog bilingualism competency and also grow this bilingualism as a core competency requirement for the present and future workforce.

In the technological era of the twenty-first century, organizations must achieve higher levels of organizational resilience. Whereas each organization will be different, there are similarities to organizational constructs and therefore looking at each of the aspects and Theory 1, in conjunction with other categorical findings, will be beneficial. Organizations should take a forward-leaning step for their organization's security management; reading this book is a good start. Building resilience not only protects an organization and its direct assets, but also the supply chain and other organizational connections, such as its inherent mission and function. Results of my original study, which inspired this book, indicated that building organizational resilience is directly related to reducing risk and specifically ensuring that acceptable risk is both understood and known by those who must make informed decisions. Decisions are made by all employees, and this includes the expanded understanding of an employee to include surrogate employee (temporary, volunteer), or a third party (such as a contractor, service provider, vendor, or inside user of a product or service).

There is a much greater control that organizations have to specifically reduce incidents of unintended insider threat through a deliberate approach to identifying specific threats unique to their organization and develop targeted risk mitigation strategy and implementation actions to mitigate risks and overall impact of external threat against organization. Human–computer threat must be managed and controlled as all employees are a piece of insider threat. Even small errors of the virtuous, or work-arounds of the wicked, can lead to larger consequences if vulnerability is created and an entry point remains open and intrusion remains undetected. Understanding human behavior within the work environment is key to prevention.

All employees may be higher risk, at various points in their positions or careers, time is a factor. Suitability of employment may change, and this should be assessed on an ongoing basis. Life struggles may creep up, including divorce, bereavement, financial strains, even the increasing prevalence of substance addiction from opioids. Employee assistance programs can be beneficial to build personal resilience and reduce the buildup of anger that can lead to deliberate vengeful or malicious actions. If your organization has experienced suicides of employees or other acts of violence, a close reassessment of support mechanisms and how to reduce this risk should be completed quickly. Suicide, and the potential for active shooter events, may be part of the threat to your risk landscape.

Vengeful acts have unintended consequences, and vengeful acts may not necessarily target the organization directly, but could be made upon a supervisor, or other employee for personal reasons. Malicious acts are primarily intended to be malicious, but must also be considered as an unintended insider threat, because doors can also be left opened becoming a vulnerability for other intrusions. All insiders are a threat to organizations; this theoretical model provides a base for expanding an organization's conceptualization of who insiders are and how the threat exists. A question that might be asked is this: What is being done in each of these categories to mitigate risk? For example, one could take the 32 human-risk behavior typologies, map them to the specific categories, and determine organizationally what is being done to mitigate these behaviors. All insider threat models should address unintended insider threat, or the absence of it. Although there are some overlaps and interconnectivity, unintended insider threat is a discipline itself, and much more deliberate attention should be made in the assessment and mitigation of insider threat.

Unintended insider threat has the potential for cascading consequences both inside the organization; as well extend beyond to customers, and customers of customers. Information technology security and human risk must continue to be addressed by organizations. Organizations should consider, for the future, creating studies to look at similar and complex issues by using grounded theory and constant comparative method, and gaining lessons learned that I believe can make a critical difference to enhancing organization resilience from insider threat. For example, organizations may choose to seeking discovery from their in-house experts and try to set aside hierarchical protocols that create resistance against sharing knowledge. Yes it is time consuming, but great value can be gained through this learning process.

Ensuring that researchers are trusted is important; research in information technology typically receives lower response rates than other disciplines. This does not mean trusted simply at face value, but someone who is able to be trusted, to listen, and to appreciate the gift of knowledge that is being given to them. Incorporating the right subject matter experts into the research process is also important. Recognizing that these experts exist at multiple levels of any given organization is worthy of noting. A snowball sampling approach may be extremely helpful to recognize these in house experts and should be considered for future studies. This process may, in part, help to eliminate hierarchical bias. This is not to say that the top of a structure doesn't have subject matter experts; indeed it does. However, some of the go-to experts may be in lower-level positions, and still be expert practitioners.

Expanding an organization's understanding of vulnerabilities and consequences will be important, in order to properly mitigate everchanging threats and adjust for increases or decreases in risk based on technology, human, or other factors. Based on information technology storage capabilities and potential cascading impacts, it is possible that results or incidents may not immediately occur and may be suspended for a time. When results occur, it can also be difficult to recognize this causality. Understanding consequences along with the potential for advanced consequence assessments can create a better prepared and resilient workforce, and organization.

Building organizational resilience to human–computer threat may be approached through a number of ways, depending on the organization. They are specific social change actions that are discussed as ten possible resilience-building opportunities that were derived from the earlier results presented. These are actions for:

- Sound management principles and leadership approaches, to include knowing the organization and its people thoroughly
- Ongoing employee screening and preselection
- In-house technical practical management and information assurance
- Implementation of security controls including monitor and audit
- Promotion of security awareness culture as a core competency
- Accountability of information technology security through personnel evaluation
- Prioritization of investment in technology and telework risk management
- Building technology infrastructure to avoid new-on-old layering
- Support of infrastructure from initial build
- Storytelling

The following 10 sections address these action items in further detail.

6.2 Sound Management Principles and Leadership Approaches

This is an area that almost any organization should focus upon. Organizations are never the same day to day, diverse recruiting practice (which can be a good thing) also creates the need for increased organizational awareness of its people. Management practice should include understanding the organization, as well as the connections to the organization. Relooking at who the customer/stakeholder base is and how the workforce is connecting with it can also be increasingly valuable. Knowing the culture and behavior of the organization at large, is important to building resilience. If solutions are presented that do not fit the culture, they are more likely to fail. Organizational culture can also be shifted by events, or occurrences and managers should be very aware of this as well. There is an example of a more recent television show that focuses on the leadership of business organizations posing as an employee to learn more about their organization. Although this television program is by no means representative of all organization, it does highlight how quickly a disconnect can occur among leadership, managers, employees, and even customers. As an end result, the owner gets to see the "ground truth" of their organization from a different perspective. Even being an employee for a week probably won't get the full story, but at least these notions will be grounded at a different reality level, and not that ivory tower that I discussed earlier. Responsiveness, technical support, may come much easier to those at the higher level of an organization, where those at the lower level may be required to use unsafe/unsecure technological workarounds, for example.

Even if organizations have put into place a resilience building solution, it may soon become obsolete as the organization continues to rapidly change, especially through technology and a generational shift. This is also not to assume all generations are the same. Individually they are not, although with any sociological approach trends can be identified within particular demographic groups; however, additional barriers may exist within one group or another to achieve resilience in a particular result—being strategic with resilience also matters.

Themes for reflectivity also include staff management and setting by leadership example. For example, how management practices are conducted is important, and a difference between textbook practice and reality practice should be both understood and considered by organizations. In some cases, managers may be so task-oriented that they are unable to strategically step back and to ask the right questions of their staff, or plan far enough in advance to more strategically manage risk, including measurement of risk. This may be systemic of staffing size or growth of management responsibility in different directions.

Additionally, leaders should be setting the example. For instance, if organizational leaders ignore best security practice, others will see this and take the cue. It becomes increasingly difficult when this happens, because the importance of a specific activity related to information technology security and if not followed, cybersecurity becomes minimized and marginalized. On the other hand, doing the right thing with cybersecurity also sends a strong signal for the workforce to adhere to best security practices. Expanding the understanding of risk is, therefore, important at all levels, and especially at the most senior levels of organization where leaders can be mitigating risks by changing their behavior; this change will be noticed.

I haven't addressed social media and leadership too much; however, if we look at celebrity Twitter debacles, such as with Rosanne Barr losing her recently revitalized television series because of a distasteful tweet—one can easily see the harm that can be done not just to one's own career, but to those who rely upon the business entity. Sometimes using social media for a leader or supervisor can be just like a shovel digging one's own grave, the grave of the business, and the grave of your employees. Simply put, put the shovel down. Especially if you are angry, or under any type of alcohol or narcotic (legal or otherwise) influence, just walk away. Stay on messaging. Social media can be good—absolutely—but it needs to be more strategically thought out.

President Donald Trump, in part, probably won the election because of his persistent tweets on social media. Even if you don't agree with him, or do, ultimately, he made a connection with the people. He also kept a lot of people talking about him—a lot. I recall him wishing me a happy Mother's Day before anyone else had. Sure, it went out to hundreds of thousands of people, but it mattered. There are a lot of mothers who perhaps didn't have anyone wish them happy Mother's Day, but Donald Trump did—and first thing. I watched the social media followings numbers click up at a very rapid pace, so was not shocked when he won. President Trump has previously praised Barack Obama for running a fantastic social media campaign, and I'm very sure he had taken note of this. However, just as this has helped Trump, he has also been criticized about sharing too much, and when errors have been made, judgment has quickly followed by the masses. Donald Trump has also been plagued with having to fire various staffers for clearance suitability issues, as well as domestic violence assertions.

6.3 Employee Screening and Preselection

Organizational resilience begins, in part, before an employee is hired. This is critical to remember. Human core competencies need to be reinforced, redeveloped, or modified so that organizations may be flexible and adaptable as the work environment, including employees and technology, change. Familiar human resource core competencies, such as writing and verbal communications, should see security competencies added for cybersecurity as a prerequisite for position applications. As I have discussed, there are many human–computer threats to an organization cascading across multiple areas, and I interpret that information technology security as important enough to be a core competency for the future workforce in order to mitigate risk and effectively support operational effectiveness and retain proprietary knowledge.

The selection of candidates using preemployment screen tools (which is already frequently being used) could potentially include significantly more questions relating to knowledge of information technology security practices at large, which could factor into selection rankings. Considering the human risk of employees to the enterprise system, organizations should consider reworking their hiring practices and match them to the technological needs of today including the identification of potential behavioral traits that are undesirable, and higher risk such as extreme narcissism.

6.4 In-House Practical Management and Information Assurance

Ensuring that enough subject matter experts are readily available in-house to manage the need for day-to-day oversight and information assurance is necessary to minimize risk to an organization. On-the-spot corrections and remedial training are a part of mitigation and contribute to building organizational resilience. Having enough security experts to run coordinated physical and technological security checks on both a random and routine basis is essential. Technology will continue to play a role in this function; however, people are still required to verify that individuals complete the proper training are adhering to the rules, and to gain insight into the changing risk environment through observation and pragmatic application. Additionally, managing information security spills can be time consuming, and should be recognized when factoring in the appropriate staff size for an organization so that many of the essential functions of monitoring are not simply set aside. As technology devices in the workplace grow, the number of technicians should also expand to meet increasing demands. There may be some exceptions to this, as particular software updates may be made in the cloud. There are, however, various levels of cloud security, and this will need to be further explored.

Creating an increase in warnings and alerts to mentally prompt employees to enhance human–computer hygiene and prevent spillage to begin with is prudent. Of course, mechanisms to report incidents should also be well known. If an employee believes that they will be detected anyway, this may be an incentive for early reporting, minimizing the door opening for the intruder to enter. Incentivizing self-reporting of errors can be done, but it will take innovation.

Accidental incidents should not be without consequence; however, consideration should be given to the response action taken when this does occur. Habitual offenders should not necessarily be afforded the same consideration. Each occurrence should be tracked, and assessed for possible future prevention approaches, vulnerabilities, gaps, and mitigation or response and recovery techniques.

6.5 Implementation of Security Controls Including Monitoring and Auditing

Indeed, along with prescreening for employment, as previously discussed, the ongoing monitoring of employees at all levels of the organization is necessary. Privileged users are potentially high-risk because of the possibility that privileged users' credentials could be stolen, and then a malicious user obtains a Domain Admin account; having effective privileged access management, or a privileged user management program is critical. Ensuring that when privileges are not needed, they are removed quickly, and in some cases managing just-in-time elevated permissions can reduce the risk of privileged accounts being exploited.

From an insider threat perspective, this monitoring is also important because, as mentioned, circumstances change in the lives of employees over time for several different reasons. The insider threat is complex. On an enterprise level, there are both supervised and unsupervised software programs that can assist in detecting anomalies, that might manifest with unexpected bursts of data, or other errant patterns. In the physical space, employees may or may not display changed behavior, but managers and colleagues have an opportunity to identify stressors or other threats by becoming more aware of changes or patterns in behavior. Again, referrals to employee resources for support could minimize risk for those who may be experiencing challenges in their lives, as a form of resilience. If the culture has a stigma of employee resources, then this is something that should be tackled. Resilience can be gained through this support of people and their behavior. It is important to understand that malicious insiders were not always bad eggs or actors; many were recruited because of being disenchanted by the organization and being identified externally as a vengeful employee, often through social media, with an opportunity to exploit for reasons such as revenge, financial gain, and in some situations as seeking notoriety or infamy.

Where external-facing security is important, looking inward is also important, along with examining the potential medium where the two shall meet. Audit control systems should be used to examine process and functions and should focus on information technology security and risk that transcends human risk and physical risk. This audit function could be external, and outsourced, but the risk between outsourcing and insourcing will need to be considered. A high level of confidence and integrity needs to be sought with external contracting in information security. Are there experts that can be outsourced? Absolutely there are. Should there also be non-disclosures and other security controls, such as returning all organizational documents after the audit is complete? Yes.

6.6 Promotion of Security Awareness Culture as a Core Competency

Training, coupled with an awareness of human behavior including the 32 typologies described earlier, will be an important consideration for organizations. Preventing others from doing things that they shouldn't, even unintended, is part of this vigilance. Being diligent by staying informed, including learning about new threats, and taking personal action and accountability to minimize those threats is an employee responsibility. Ensuring that employees understand their role minimizing risk from within the system requires organizational cooperation with several functional parts of the organization to include information security, to physical security, and to personnel management. Understanding operational impacts of inappropriate behavior, as well as consequences, should be well known by employees. This may be achieved through more transparent descriptions of occurrences/incidents and related consequences or potential consequences. The incorporation of meaningful stories may assist in gaining needed awareness. Training should be ongoing. The recognition of the four various types of insider threat is also a good starting point. Recognizing that employees and surrogate employees can place an organization at risk and fall into the categories of virtuous, wicked, vengeful, and malicious is an important distinction. Recognizing risky human behavior, providing on-the-spot correction, or using referral programs can minimize unintended insider threat, in part. Programs within the organization can be scoped to minimizing risk in these four categories. An effective security awareness training and education program that includes both cybersecurity and traditional security is essential. Ideally, throughout an organization there should be permanently assigned security officers as a force multiplier of the program. There should be security experts positioned where an employee can physically bring their devices, including bring your own device (BYOD), for review to ensure that best security setting adjustments are in place.

6.7 Accountability of Information Technology Security through Personnel Evaluation

Incorporating accountability into evaluation systems may be an effective tool, especially for management and organizational leaders. Evaluation systems may have not been updated to reflect the current security environment, nor organizational value on information technology security. Both rewards and consequences should be linked to information technology security management. Consequences should link to appropriate accountability levels as developed by the organization. They should be phased in, but be meaningful enough for employees to take note of them, and make effort to adhere to them with a greater sense of urgency. In the technologically based workplace, the evaluation of information technology security effectiveness may be of value to an organization, along with training supervisors to understand their role in evaluation including in information technology security. Organizations should consider how they conduct their evaluations and how to create more meaning to them. In terms of information security, several measurements could be incorporated simply by looking at the categorical results contained in this book, which could be selected for measurement. Having organizations require supervisors to both recognize the value of information technology security for both themselves and their subordinates can go a long way in improving employee worth. Reducing risk is valuable to an organization on many levels, depending on the nature of the organization.

6.8 Prioritization of Investment in Technology and Telework Risk Management

Money is a big deal in technology prioritization; without it, information technology security will be challenged and its effectiveness impact short-changed. Bringing in requirements earlier, rather than having computer engineers left to work with what is left, will be important for organizations to consider. There is also risk in teleworking, and with what devices are used and how. Although my original research was not specifically directed toward teleworking individuals, there are also risks surrounding this practice, and these risks should be directly addressed by organizations. The removal of large volumes of data from an organization, whether taken from a brick-and-mortar site or off-site, should be examined. Even small data, trade secrets should be protected behind additional layers of security. Human behavior, as well as infrastructure support, must be geared to minimize threat that may be created by teleworking. This threat will vary by organization but could include loss of proprietary knowledge, or introducing compromise into the enterprise system. Threat of theft of physical items is also potentially a higher risk in less-secure spaces of one's home. Using a home computer, shared by others in a home, for telework is not optimal and may be a risk.

Instead, organizational-supported technology that can be brought into the workplace for reimaging, other monitoring, and updating is ideal. For example, users could have encrypted computers to guard against physical compromise if stolen from home, along with having the proper office equipment, such as recommended shredders that meet security standards. The risks surrounding printing documents was described briefly; however, there is risk in printing from an enterprise system, as well as a risk for not printing, because employees may be more susceptible for loss if they carry hard-copy documents back and forth. Printing specifically should not be ignored and will likely vary by organization. There is risk in proprietary information loss as well in telework since direct monitoring is difficult. The risks and benefits should be weighed. Telework can be an important recruitment incentive for top talent, as well as allowing for flexibility for a diverse workforce. A lot of jobs have shifted to be 100 percent remote, and this can create a complexity of issues. Ensuring that these teleworkers do not have elevated status beyond what is needed, and that they still have monitoring, will be important. I'm not advocating the demise of telework; the future of telework is here, and I seriously doubt we will shift backward. However, additional investment to mitigate risk to organizations as a result of teleworking needs to occur.

6.9 Building Technology Infrastructure to Avoid New-on-Old Layering Risk

Organizations should assess their systems and identify mission-critical functions that rely on main or critical systems. The introduction of new technology may be layered onto older platforms, and this could be a risk. Organizations should ask themselves how this layering could impact their organization and how they should approach assessment and risk management practice. New technology may also be at higher risk because the vulnerabilities may not have yet been identified but are identified through time by the vendor or manufacturer. The ideology that something is new so it is better may not be true. There may also be risks to new technology relying on old technology that was not designed to protect against new technological threat. For example, control systems through wireless access may be vulnerable. Systems that may be ultimately accessed by wireless networks should be known and tested. However, it is possible for systems to be accessed through wireless communications that may not be visible to organizations and may pose a higher risk. Employees may unintentionally create these wireless connections, especially if computer network connections are not locked down.

6.10 Support of Infrastructure from Initial Build

When systems are initially established or built, a threat exists that someone could establish compromise, though this is more likely to be intentional. Computer engineers as well as physical security should monitor setups, and not simply rely on contractors or employees to do the right thing without specific governance. A trusted supply chain is critical, and this needs to be determined in advance, depending on the acquisition type. If a new build-out occurs, it is possible that either physical or virtual backdoors could be set up without an organization knowing about it. Loss would depend on the nature of the organization; however, loss could be critical or place a business out of the market share if intellectual capital is released.

6.11 Storytelling

Storytelling is an opportunity for organizations to make meaningful connections that transcend the cyber-physical domain and strategically communicate across hierarchical structures and the breadth and depth of organizations. A pilot study within an organization could, for example, be designed to measure how people learn technology security within an organization by teaching two groups—one with meaningful storytelling and one without storytelling. Although storytelling is effective, perhaps understanding the how authentic storytelling within a particular organizational culture is also valuable as a tool for cultural change.

Within this subject matter of insider threat—whereas organizations will differ in their purpose or mission set—the need for cyber-physical digital-analog bilingualism is necessary to minimize risk and create opportunities to inform decision making at not just the operational level, but at all levels. This cyber-physical digital-analog bilingualism can contribute to the knowledge of what is or is not acceptable risk for a particular organization. Stories need to be told so a risk-informed culture can be created and sustained. If true stories are not provided, they will be made up and might be well off the mark of what the business brand should be. It is best to provide stories that are grounded in reality that can teach lessons in information technology security to which a user can relate. Stories, if properly told, can help to alter behavior for the good of the organization, correct inaccuracies, and reimage.

6.12 Final Note

I'm so glad I have been able to share the more accurately informed story of the insider threat; assessment and mitigation of risks. I believe that this book has helped you, by enveloping you with practical knowledge, and now you will no doubt be able to more effectively conduct an assessment and mitigation of risks. The threat will continue to exist, but the mitigation of the risks are very possible, especially if the threat is approached more holistically, with the enhanced interdisciplinary approach including the sociological lenses.

In closing, I ask one last question of you—have you seen the typical insider threat lately? Answer: Take a look in the mirror and then tilt the mirror toward the person to your right and your left, even the one behind you who might be shoulder surfing you. If you don't have a mirror, just use your mobile selfie feature. Then, armed with your knowledge, spring into action. You can be the change agent your organization has been looking for!

Endnote

1. Award Winning Hurricane Tracking Software (2018). Retrieved from www.hurricanesoftware.com.

Index

Note: Page numbers in italic and bold refer to figures and tables, respectively.

Printed in the United States
by Baker & Taylor Publisher Services

Printed in the United States
by Baker & Taylor Publisher Services